# GEORGE MICHAEL

FIRST PUBLISHED IN THE UNITED STATES OF AMERICA IN 2017 by:
Lesser Gods
15 W. 36th St., 8th Fl., New York, NY 10018
An imprint of Overamstel Publishers, Inc.
PHONE (646) 850-4201
www.lessergodsbooks.com

*Published simultaneously in the United Kingdom by*
*John Blake Publishing Ltd*

DISTRIBUTED BY: Consortium Book Sales & Distribution
34 13th Ave. NE #101, Minneapolis, MN 55413
PHONE (800) 283-3572
www.cbsd.com

FIRST EDITION April 2017 / 10 9 8 7 6 5 4 3 2 1
PRINTED AND BOUND IN THE U.S.A.
ISBN: 978-1944713263
LIBRARY OF CONGRESS CONTROL NUMBER: 2017933769

# GEORGE MICHAEL

## THE LIFE 1963–2016

### EMILY HERBERT

LESSER
GODS

# CONTENTS

# DEATH OF
# AN ICON

Christmas Day 2016. Many were just sitting down to dinner when the news came through. One of the most famous stars of his generation had passed away. Aged just fifty-three, George Michael, golden boy of the 1980s and international superstar for the whole of his adult life, had been found dead in bed at his home in Goring-on-Thames, Oxfordshire, yet another high-profile death in what had been an extraordinary year.

Ever since the singer David Bowie had died at the beginning of 2016, a roll call of the musical greats had seemed to follow suit: Prince, Leonard Cohen, Earth, Wind & Fire founder Maurice White, Beatles producer George Martin, Keith Emerson, Merle Haggard—the list seemed to go on and on. Many more famous figures from other walks of life, including the writer Harper Lee, the actor Alan Rickman, the Egyptian politician Boutros Boutros-

Ghali and numerous others had gone, too, which, allied to a series of earth-shattering world events in the political sphere—Brexit, the election of Donald Trump, ructions in the Eurozone and the ongoing turmoil in the Middle East—had seemed to be changing the very nature of the planet. And now, adding to the roll call of the Grim Reaper's subjects in this extraordinary year, there was George Michael, too.

There seemed to be something particularly tragic about George's death, however—a man who, like Prince, had gone decades before his time. A generation had grown up with music from his Wham! days as a backdrop to their lives and had watched, with a good deal of sympathy, albeit laced with bewilderment, as he battled his demons in later years, with addictions to alcohol and drugs leading to all manner of public escapades in which a worse-for-wear George would find himself in the headlines yet again. All this was actually explained by the battle that the public was not privy to in the early days: the struggle George had with his homosexuality, his reluctance to go public about it for fear of upsetting his Greek Cypriot parents and, when he first hit the limelight, his fans.

George had found fame as a teen idol appealing to young girls and the record industry was none too keen on the idea of its latest heart-throb making it clear to his female fans that his interests lay very much elsewhere; and so it took the singer-songwriter years before he was eventually able to come out of the closet, which he did only when in reality he had no other choice after his arrest in 1998 for "engaging in a lewd act"—although in fairness, in later years he claimed this was a "subconsciously deliberate act." It certainly put an end to years of speculation about the true nature of his sexuality. But as with so many of his travails, this too was greeted sympathetically by a public who had come to understand that George Michael was a deeply troubled man. Although prone to complain about the excessive media coverage that resulted in such scrutiny of his life, he was at the same time a much-loved figure and there was a palpable desire for George to defeat his demons once and for all.

Alas, it was never going to happen and soon the sad news of his demise had been verified. "It is with great sadness that we can confirm our beloved son, brother and friend George passed away peacefully at home over the Christmas period," his publicist Connie Filippello said in a statement. "The family would ask that their privacy be respected at this difficult and emotional time. There will be no further comment at this stage." Of course, there was a great deal of speculation as to what actually happened: George's heavy drug use was no secret and it was also widely known that he had spent periods in rehab, none of which had ever managed to make much of a difference to his life. Many feared the worst, but it eventually emerged that the cause of death had been heart failure: he died "in bed, lying peacefully," his manager Michael Lippman said. "I'm devastated," he added, but there was "no foul play whatsoever." Even so, George's lifestyle, specifically his drug intake, must have taken its toll and it is the case that cardiac arrest is frequently suffered by heroin users. There were persistent rumors that this had become George's drug of choice although members of his family strongly denied it. There was no doubt, however, that he had spent long periods in rehab and had indulged mightily in narcotics over the years.

The police had been called to the property as is standard in these matters and released a statement just before midnight on December 25, 2016: "Thames Valley Police were called to a property in Goring-on-Thames shortly before 2 p.m. Christmas Day. Sadly, a 53-year-old man was confirmed deceased at the scene. At this stage the death is being treated as unexplained but not suspicious." An ambulance had arrived at around 1:40 p.m. and the reality began to sink in for those on the scene: George Michael was gone.

Of course, George had had health problems for years, one of the most serious being a bout of pneumonia in 2011, during which he'd needed a tracheotomy and which had left him with permanent lung damage, serious for a man who had previously confessed to smoking twenty-five marijuana joints a day. There was some speculation that there might have been some form of recurrence, this time a fatal one. "His lungs never fully recovered," one source explained. "That can happen after a serious bout of pneumonia like George had. Sometimes, it leaves the lung scarred or damaged, which can lead to a loss of function. It can leave you feeling breathless, as the lungs have a smaller capacity than before. George made no secret about how much he smoked. Smoking can seriously affect the lungs and dramatically increases the risk of infection. After having pneumonia, it's incredibly dangerous to smoke at all." George had in fact previously given up smoking but some reports were suggesting that he had taken up the habit again.

As more details began to filter through about what had really happened, it emerged that it was George's boyfriend, the celebrity hairstylist Fadi Fawaz, who had found the singer. Fadi was clearly in a state of shock. "ITs a xmas i will never forget finding your partner dead peacefully in bed first thing in the morning. I will never stop missing you xx," he tweeted. George's ex-partner, with whom he had been for many years (and many thought a reunion was on the cards), Kenny Goss, also issued a statement: "He was a major part of my life and I loved him very, very much. The beautiful memories and music he brought to the world will always be an important part of my life and those who also loved and admired him."

Others were quick to follow suit to pay tribute and their respects. Sir Elton John, with whom George had fallen out on and off over the course of several years, but with whom he was now thought to be on much warmer terms, wrote: "I am in deep shock. I have lost a beloved friend—the kindest, most generous soul and a brilliant artist. My heart goes out to his family and all of his fans. @GeorgeMichael #RIP."

Equally poignant was a posting from George's Wham!

bandmate Andrew Ridgeley, with whom he'd found fame all those many years ago. "Heartbroken at the loss of my beloved friend Yog [George's nickname]. Me, his loved ones, his friends, the world of music, the world at large. 4ever loved. A xx." Indeed, the two of them had shared a particularly special bond—no one else could have known quite what it was like for those two young boys still barely out of their teens to be catapulted into the spotlight and onto the stage of international stardom. Ridgeley had long since bowed out from the mayhem and lived a quiet life in semi-retirement but, on the few occasions he did venture out, it was frequently connected to George, as when he took part in *George Michael: A Different Story*, a 2005 TV documentary about the life of his old friend. There was clearly still a huge amount of affection there.

It wasn't just people who knew George who were affected by the news, however, and as sometimes happens after a very public death, private stories were emerging that testified to what a decent man he had been. A public tide of grief was swelling and along with it numerous reports of George's kindness and generosity. "A woman on *Deal Or No Deal* told us she needed £15,000 for IVF treatment. George Michael secretly phoned the next day and gave her the £15,000," said the television presenter Richard Osman. It emerged that George had also given a barmaid an $8,500 tip on learning she was a student nurse with debts, while charities including the Terrence Higgins Trust and Macmillan Cancer Support revealed that the singer had secretly donated millions of pounds to them.

NHS nurses who attended a free concert that Michael held for them in 2006 were keen that the world should know of his generosity. "No one had ever done anything like that before, and no one has done it since," Caroline Smith, thirty-seven, a senior nurse at Royal Surrey County Hospital, told *The Times*. "It was such a powerful evening. For somebody as famous as that, to thank us in such a way, was really quite inspirational. I should hope at the very least he's in everybody's thoughts."

Fellow nurse Simon Pawlin added: "It set him apart. We left that concert buzzing. The fact that it wasn't for the cameras, it wasn't about him being a celebrity, it was about him giving something back, that tells you something about the person he was. It was a very special evening we'll never forget."

It further emerged that George donated the royalties from "Jesus To A Child" to children's charity Childline, a gift that amounted to £2 million, on condition that it be kept secret. "George helped us to reach out to hundreds of thousands of children through his generosity," said Childline founder Esther Rantzen, who was among those calling for a tribute concert in his honour and who believed his personal issues might have contributed to a special sympathy for the children that needed Childline.

"He approached us, rather than us going cap in hand to him, but it was an intensely personal gift. He didn't want it to be known or to be part of his image. I think it would be wonderful to celebrate him with a tribute concert next year. We were able to counsel 300,000 children who needed help last year, through emails, online and phone calls, and George made a palpable difference. There was a sense of personal interest. He kept his sexuality quiet and it may have been tough for him when he was younger."

By this time, George's death was making headlines worldwide. Fans and admirers began leaving floral tributes outside his home overlooking the River Thames, which still had a berry-and apple-covered wreath on one side door and two reindeer statues in the garden covered with fairy lights, while an outpouring of affection and sorrow was engulfing everyone involved with his private life. "The family and close friends of George have been touched beyond words by the incredible outpouring of love for him in the hours and days since his death," his publicist said in a further statement, which was also keen to emphasize that the death was not drug-related. "For someone whose life was ultimately about his music and the love he had for his family and friends, his fans and the world at large, there could be no more fitting tribute than the many, many, kind words that have been said and the numerous plays his records have received. Contrary to some reports, there were no suspicious circumstances surrounding his death, and from the bottom of our hearts we thank those who, rightly, have chosen to celebrate his life and legacy at this most distressing of times."

More people were now paying tribute. Sir Paul McCartney, who had worked with George on "Heal The

Pain," said: "George Michael's sweet soul music will live on even after his sudden death. Having worked with him on a number of occasions his great talent always shone through and his self-deprecating sense of humor made the experience even more pleasurable."

Fellow eighties pop idol Boy George, who had also had his fair share of public problems and the occasional disagreement with George, wrote: "He was so loved and I hope he knew it because the sadness today is beyond words. Devastating."

And Robbie Williams, whose first solo single was a cover of Michael's song "Freedom," and who had also had a well-documented battle with alcohol, wrote: "Oh God no …I love you George …Rest In Peace x."

The only note of discord was struck by the DJ Andy Kershaw, who clearly did not understand quite how popular George Michael was with the public, or quite the strength of feeling his death had produced. He provoked a very angry reaction when, in a Facebook post that was later deleted, he warned people to, "brace yourselves for the now routine hysterical over-reaction and obligatory bogus sentimentality which always—these days—follows the unfortunate premature deaths of these figures, regardless of how flimsy, insignificant and lightweight their cultural contribution happened to be. Please spare me the predictable onion from the pocket outpourings, claiming he was 'one of the greats.' No, he was not. (Really? Up there with Louis Armstrong, Johnny Cash, Joni Mitchell, Hank Williams,

Jimi Hendrix, Robert Johnson, Van Morrison? I could go on.) George Michael was in reality a very successful yet frivolous, glib, and fleeting pop star. Can we keep a sense of proportion?"

Fans were not slow to react. "Do us a favor, Andy, can you publish the list of artists it would be OK to grieve, just in case we get it wrong again," Bruce Keith Miller remarked. Meanwhile, Abigail Dombey was livid: "I thought you were great when I was young, now I know you're a bitter, angry man. George Michael was worth a hundred of you." Others voiced similar sentiments at what was an extremely unpopular view. Sara Anne Lambert wrote: "He is still someone's brother and son, Andy. Think about how you would feel reading your status about one of your loved ones. Not necessary!" And Lenny Lovett opined: "A particularly unpleasant post. I've no opinion on the chap either way but to demean his death in such sad circumstances is just nasty and unnecessary." No one was slow to point out that Kershaw himself had had some serious personal problems in the past.

Meanwhile, George's partner Fadi Fawaz was also giving more details about what had happened and quite how suddenly this had come out of the blue. "We were supposed to be going for Christmas lunch," he told the *Daily Telegraph*. "I went round there to wake him up and he was just gone, lying peacefully in bed. We don't know what happened yet. Everything had been very complicated recently, but George was looking forward to Christmas, and so was I. Now everything is ruined. I want people to remember him the way he was. He was a beautiful person." That reference to complications might well have meant Texan art dealer Kenny Goss, with whom George had spent thirteen years before their split in 2011 and with whom he had recently been in touch, leading many to speculate that they might once more become an item.

What was also beginning to emerge was quite how reclusive George had become in recent years, not least, according to many, because his appearance had changed so much from the days when he was a handsome young gun, all deep tan and gleaming white teeth, complete with a mop of flicky, golden-streaked hair. "He changed over the years, got a lot bigger and wore glasses," the manager of a nearby pub, who wanted to remain anonymous, told the *Daily Telegraph*. "He was very self-conscious. He just did not look like George Michael any more. It's very sad. I went down to lay a candle outside his house with a group and they said the last time he was seen was watching the torchlight procession on Christmas Eve from the window." Nor had George been seen at Midnight Mass on Christmas Eve, which it had been his habit to attend. According to a London neighbor, he had been looking "tired" and "haggard." "I remember thinking he looked unwell," Sasha Gretsay told the *Mirror*. "He looked worried and older than my friend who was 57."

Nonetheless, there had been some hard partying going on chez George, reclusive or not, and there were further fears that this might have fatally undermined his health. "George loved having friends over and was often still going strong well into the following morning," one source said. "This continued right up until his death. He may have been in his 50s but it's fair to say he gave much younger partygoers a run for their money and the atmosphere was always quite hedonistic."

Of course, George died a very rich man. At the time of his death he was estimated to be worth about £105 million, with his house—called Mill Cottage—in Oxfordshire worth £5 million, a property in Highgate, North London, worth about £8 million, a £3.5-million beach home in Sydney and a £2.5-million house in Los Angeles. He also had an art collection, with pieces by Banksy and Tracey Emin, and a Damien Hirst glass tank containing a calf, which he'd bought for £3.5 million in 2007.

George had two sisters, Melanie and Yioda, and numerous godchildren, including former Spandau Ballet bassist Martin Kemp's offspring, Roman and Harley. He was particularly close to Melanie, who was left £50 million in his will, with sums going out to his other sister and the godchildren. These included the offspring of his cousin and friend Andros Georgiou, who he had grown up with but with whom there had been a serious rift.

George was godfather to Andros's two children, Harry and the TV reality star James Kennedy. He had been Andros's best man when he married wife Jackie in 1991, but the two men had in fact kept one another at a distance for the best part of two decades after disagreements about George's lifestyle. Ironically, however, they had agreed to meet just one week on from when George died, a meeting and proper reconciliation that could now, obviously, never take place.

"He was feeling better about things and had stopped all the naughty stuff," Andros told the *Sun*. "But there was so much pain in his heart, I think it just gave up. He felt like he had let people down, when of course he hadn't at all—he was the people's superstar. We both felt it was time [to meet]. We would have hugged, probably both have said sorry, then got on with it. I used to say I didn't want the next time I see Yog to be at his graveside but now that's exactly what's going to happen. I'm heartbroken. When we were 20, 21, he used to say he'd die young. I'd say, 'Don't be stupid, what are you talking about?' Now he's gone, it's devastating."

Andros's son, James, was similarly devastated, revealing he hadn't seen George for a decade before he died. "He was like a second dad but we never really got to talk again, which is heartbreaking," he told the *Sun*. "That really upset me the most. I always thought that once I get older, make a little money to travel myself, I could just go find him. It was a matter of people being stubborn and thinking there was more time than there actually is. I know he was sick for a while. I was crying all night when I heard the news. He is a legend and he touched everyone with his music. I love him and I'll always love him."

Of course, although James knew his godfather was a very famous man, he was party to both the public and the private side of his life. "He was a massive inspiration—the way he moved, the way he dressed, the way he danced, wrote," he said. "Just everything about George was incredible. He would spend every Christmas with us [in the family home in Hampstead] till the age of about ten and then we moved. He got me a rocking horse and that Barney the dinosaur that year. He was great—I used to call him Uncle George. He was like a second dad—he was family. He wasn't George Michael to me, it was family. His Christmas song would be playing in the kitchen when we were there and I didn't even know it was him. It was always fun when George was there. He would always bring the best presents. His energy really set the tone for our family."

The estrangement was also believed by many to have taken a terrible toll on George himself. For someone who attracts so much public attention, a close personal inner circle can be a lifeline, and for a significant part of it to disappear can be a terrible blow.

Kyriakos Pourikou, the husband of George's cousin, Andros's sister Katerina, was equally shell-shocked, and given that so many people were now talking openly about George's problems with drugs revealed that all the speculation was putting an increased layer of tension on the family at the worst possible time. "We're hearing old stories again and again," Kyriacos told the *Mirror*. "If you know him, he's different. You hear the bad things about him but it's part of being a rock star. I've never seen that [heroin use], we're family. Did I ever see him on drugs? Not while we've been together. We knew he wasn't well but not how bad. We just heard it like everybody else at eleven o'clock at night. He was a great cousin, a great philanthropist, a great man. It's a great loss to everyone. He was a very generous person. I think in a few years we'll find out what we've missed. I know he's been going through some tough times but it's sad it's happened on Christmas Day."

Pourikou was another to know the public and private George. "He's touched everybody's hearts over the 25 years that I've known him," he said sadly. "I feel very humble to know this guy. It's just a waste of a life, 53. We're just waiting to see what's going to happen and when the funeral will be." Of the split with Andros, he commented, "They were a big part of each other's life from the age of 18 to their mid-30s when they fell out. He came over to meet up and tried to gear himself up to meet him but it never happened. He loved him so much and that's when things went downhill. They were good together. I think they needed each other."

Fadi Fawaz continued to grieve: not only had George been his partner, he had also found the body and was now having to come to terms with his loss. He went on to raise a few eyebrows, however, when he shared a "lost song" of George's, "This Kind Of Love," from the unfinished album, *Trojan Souls*, on Twitter. Thought to have been co-produced with Elton John in the early 1990s, it contained the line: "This empty house seems to get colder and colder. So won't you stay here with me?" The song was, in fact, already available on YouTube, but it prompted an angry reaction from some people, who felt that George and George alone should decide what music was to be released. Not least from Andrew Ridgeley, who tweeted: "No, #GM controlled all his output. I, nor anyone else have the right to transgress that principle."

Fadi had written "my baby" beside the track but other fans got in on the act, arguing about whether music that George had previously been working on but had left unreleased should ever see the light of day. He was a known perfectionist and, sometimes to the frustration of his fans, would give up on tracks if he thought they weren't good enough. "George was a talented and brilliant musician but he could be obstinate and difficult because he was such a perfectionist," a source told the *Mirror*. However, given that he was never going to produce any more music, there was a clear desire on the part of some people to hear what was actually already there.

George's family, however, was furious, and after an intervention from senior lawyer John Reid of Russells Solicitors, the link was taken down. "This song is unreleased… our client did not wish, and his estate do not wish, this song to be publicly available," he said in a stiffly worded letter to Fawaz. "The exploitation of this song, including the posting of hyperlinks to unauthorised reproductions of the song, is an infringement of our client's rights."

Fadi complied but was equally livid in return, tweeting: "The song I posted was found online they [*sic*] are many versions of it, please do your research if u think u r professional in what u do." Ironically, one of the reasons it was never released in the first place was thought to be due to another legal tussle, but feelings were still raw and the matter caused a good deal of upset.

With no George around to adjudicate, it was very difficult to tell what he would have wanted. For a start, it turned out that he had in fact been working on new material and was planning a comeback in 2017. Before George died, the music producer Naughty Boy had given an interview to the BBC in which he said, "I can't wait. I don't know what to expect. And, to be honest, he's more mysterious than anyone else so I'm actually excited. I reached out and then he got back. He's got an album coming out next year and he's going to be doing something for my album as well." But what the state of play with the album was, and whether it had been completed, was not clear; what was known, however, was that there were three full albums of music in his private collection that had never been released.

On 27 December, it was reported that the family had announced that George would be buried beside his mother, Lesley Panayiotou, at the family plot in Highgate Cemetery, North London. George had been devastated by her death from cancer in 1997, yet another burden in a life that had sometimes seemed too full of them. "Everyone in the family is struggling to take it in but at least he's finally at rest with his mum now," said Katerina Pourikou. The world continued to grieve, however. So just what was it about a boy from a North London Greek Cypriot family that inspired such love and loyalty and blazed quite so brightly as a bona fide star?

## 2

# THE LITTLE GREEK BOY

In 1953, Kyriacos Panayiotou, a Greek Cypriot restaurateur-to-be, decided to seek his fortunes abroad. He alighted upon the idea of coming to England: there were opportunities there and Cyprus was at the time a British colony, although independence was fast approaching. Indeed, the campaign to gain independence from the UK meant that violent demonstrations were not unknown, which in turn, ironically, encouraged more Cypriots to emigrate. Kyriacos was one of them: he made his way from his warm Mediterranean home to cold and rainy England and started work as a waiter while he planned what was to come next.

Kyriacos changed his name to the slightly more Anglicized Jack Panos and met and married Lesley Angold Harrison, an English dancer from a working-class background, in Finchley, North London. They started their family: first, little Yioda arrived, followed shortly afterwards by Melanie. This was a Greek Cypriot family, however, and so when their third child arrived on June 25, 1963, the couple were beside themselves with delight that they now had a son. Georgios Kyriacos, named after his father, was from day one the much-cherished baby of the family, a status that for all the wealth and fame he later accrued, he never really lost.

The Panos family were to see an enormous change in their circumstances but they were not wealthy when George came along and were in fact living above a launderette in a working-class area of East Finchley, North London. Jack worked long hours as he sought to better himself and it began to work: he was promoted to restaurant manager.

When George was still small the family moved to a house in the leafy borough of Kingsbury, where the young George would play in Roe Green Park. He remembered this period of his life and his first day at school in the song "Round Here," George's version of "Penny Lane," with the accompanying video filmed in the area: "I hear my mama call in Kingsbury Park," he sang in a touching recollection of his childhood. He was to attend Kingsbury High School until the Panos family once more moved on when he was in his early teens.

For someone who is thought of as quintessentially Anglo-Greek, it might surprise some to learn that George Michael was technically Jewish. His maternal grandmother was

Jewish but given that she lived during the time of World War Two and the Holocaust, the international political climate made her nervous about disclosing her roots even though she was resident in the UK, where no threat to the Jewish community existed. She married a non-Jew and brought up her children, including George's mother, with no knowledge of their real origins and sent Lesley to a convent school in order to cover all tracks. The truth only emerged much later.

"She thought if they didn't know their mother was Jewish they wouldn't be at risk," George told the *Los Angeles Times* in 2008. But Judaism goes down through the maternal line, not the paternal, which means that George is also Jewish, something he has been happy to acknowledge. In 2001, he visited Israel to attend a wedding in Tel Aviv, that of the British photographer and album designer Simon Halfon, who was marrying Israeli Anat Browerman. He did so at a time when many other celebrities were avoiding the Middle East, given the ongoing tensions, and it is also notable that at the time of his death his long-term partner, Fadi Fawaz, was a Muslim, albeit a very Westernized one.

But when George was a child of course all that lay ahead. He adored his mother and they were very close until her untimely death from cancer, aged sixty, in 1997. Because his father worked such long hours elsewhere, George didn't actually see very much of him and so it was to his mother to whom he would turn: "My father was the typical Greek who comes to London and works 24 hours a day, so his views were never impressed on me when I was very young," he explained in *Wham! Confidential: The Death of a Supergroup*, published in 1987. "I always saw it through my mother's eyes in terms of what I should be after, and it wasn't money."

But life wasn't easy in those early years. Both parents had to work very hard: "Work was their religion," George told the *Huffington Post* in an interview in February 2009. His parents were "just constantly exhausted. They were both working so hard to get us where they wanted us to but that made them authoritarian... I was never praised, never held. So it was not exactly the Little House on the Prairie. It really wasn't." This was a theme that was to develop in George's mind as he grew older and it really appears that the tensions came later on, when he was in his teens and decided he wanted to be a pop star; the infant George was doted on by his mother and older sisters. It was a typical close-knit Greek Cypriot family and remained so even after George became stratospherically famous and encountered his own well-documented problems along the way.

Even as a small boy, George knew that he enjoyed freedoms his elder sisters did not. "I have a huge propensity for guilt because I was a boy in a Greek family who could do what he liked from a very early age—and did because the culture was patriarchal and to indulge the boy," he told presenter Kirsty Young when he appeared on BBC Radio 4's *Desert Island Discs* in 2007. "I have two wonderful sisters, who never got their way as young Greek girls obviously.

And I grew up with terrible feelings of guilt. I had feelings of guilt as a small child, knowing that I was always the one that was going to get the easy ride. I carried that propensity for guilt in the strangest ways and I think I finally realized that one of the reasons my life has been so extreme and so self-destructive—it sounds arrogant but I never had any feeling that my talent was going to let me down." At that stage, however, he had not yet discovered that talent. All he knew was that he was a much-loved little boy who could get away with playing up in a way that his sisters could not.

Money was certainly an issue in the Panos family in the early days and both parents had to work. Even though she had children, Lesley also held down two jobs, including a stint at a chip shop, which she loathed because, "she was obsessively clean and she could never get the smell of fish out of her hair or off her skin, no matter how hard she scrubbed," said George in the *Huffington Post* interview. Things would naturally become easier when George entered his teens, but at that stage life was tough.

George was musical from very early on, although he himself had several explanations as to how this came about. According to him, it was his mother who was responsible for sparking his interest in music: coming from a show-business background herself, no matter how much her circumstances might have changed, she perhaps understood this aspect of life more than his father did. "I'd got the singing bug when I was seven, and Mum had given me a tape recorder as a present. As I got older, Dad was against the idea [of pursuing a career in music] but Mum began to realize that I might have something and started to sympathize with me," he recalled in the same interview. That was an understatement. George's father was fiercely against the idea that his son might be a musician: of immigrant stock himself and starting out as poor when he moved to the UK, the last thing he wanted was for the boy of the family to go into an area as insecure as show business. This was to lead, over and over, to clashes as George grew up and it became apparent his ambitions to become a pop star were not going to go away.

Other people also remember the importance this tape recorder had in George's life. As a young child George's closest friend was David Mortimer (later known as David Austin), who would also enjoy a career in the music industry as a songwriter and, in fact, worked with George when they were adults. He, too, remembers the tape-recorder episode although he put it at a slightly different age. "We grew up in the same street and met because our mothers were pushing us up the road in our prams and stopped to have a chat," David once said, as quoted in the *Daily Mirror*. "As children we played together all the time. We'd write songs and record them on a tape recorder. When we were about six, we did one called 'The Music Maker of the World.' How prophetic was that?"

Even so, George believed that it was actually an accident that set him off towards a career in the music industry, as it profoundly changed his interests and the way he interacted with the world. "At the age of about eight I had a head injury and I know it sounds bizarre and unlikely, but it was quite a bad bang, and I had it stitched up and stuff, but all my interests changed, everything changed in six months," he told *Desert Island Discs*.

"I had been obsessed with insects and creepy crawlies. I used to get up at five o'clock in the morning and go out into this field behind our garden and collect insects before everyone else got up and, suddenly, all I wanted to know about was music. It just seemed a very, very strange thing. And I have a theory that maybe it was something to do with this accident, this whole left-brain, right-brain thing. Nobody in my family seemed to notice but I became absolutely obsessed with music and everything changed after that."

At first this obsession merely took the form of a hobby, with George becoming an expert on everything pop-related, although as an adult he has claimed that he knew he wanted to be a pop star even back then.

Over the decades, George was to come out with mixed views on his childhood—on the one hand talking about being utterly indulged as a boy and on the other saying there wasn't much encouragement from his father, at least. But he was unequivocal in the respect he felt for his father when he was young. Jack Panos was beginning to reap the rewards from his hard work and the fact that the family finances had improved drastically from the base point of about zero was a source of great pride for his son. "I didn't learn about hard work from my father because I could never work as hard as he did," George told the *Daily Mirror* in 1996. "What he has done is more of an achievement than anything I've ever done. The idea of coming to a foreign country with nothing, working until your fingers bleed, raising your kids and getting to the point where you have a beautiful home in the countryside—that's heroic for me."

By the time George was in his teens, the family finances had improved so much—his father now owned the restaurant Angus Pride in Edgware, Middlesex—that they moved to a large house in Radlett in Hertfordshire and his parents were able to ask him if he would like to attend a private school. But George turned down the offer and went to Bushey Meads School in Hertfordshire instead. It was to prove a truly fateful decision. Early on he met a fellow pupil and the two of them clicked immediately, bonding over a shared love of pop music and much more. That fellow pupil was Andrew Ridgeley, affable and outgoing and everything the young George back then was not. Nor were George's parents 100 per cent delighted about their son's new friend: it was Andrew who was the ambitious one at that stage, Andrew who was determined to become famous in the field of either football or pop, and Andrew who encouraged George to think about becoming a professional singer. For Jack, in particular, it seemed he was encouraging George to follow the wrong path.

Andrew John Ridgeley was born on January 26, 1963 in Windlesham, Surrey, in a remarkably similar set-up to his new friend: his mother, Jenny, a teacher, is English, but his father, Albert, who worked for Canon, was also of immigrant descent—in his case Italian and Egyptian. The Ridgeleys moved to Bushey, Hertfordshire, where the young Andrew was enrolled in Bushey Meads School, a secondary school with a sixth form. When they were both twelve, he was introduced to a plump little Greek Cypriot boy whose family had just moved to the area. Andrew, who at that age was by far the cooler of the two lads, volunteered to look after the new boy and they hit it off from the start.

They were an unlikely duo: George was pudgy, shy and bespectacled; Andrew was outgoing, popular and charismatic. But they had the indefinable chemistry between them that can never be fully explained and that would result in one of the most successful double acts in the history of pop. So what was it that drew them together? In recent years great emphasis has been placed on the importance of smell when it comes to relationships—all relationships, not just romantic ones, for in this case Andrew really was what George initially seemed to be, namely very interested in girls. But perhaps their success and compatibility can be put down to one simple factor: they liked the way each other smelled.

In later years, as their lives moved in different directions, the closeness they shared as children inevitably dissipated but there was still a bond. And for all that it was George who was to enjoy stratospheric success, to the very end

Andrew retained a slightly protective aura where his former bandmate was concerned, as when he objected loudly to the unauthorized release of tracks recorded years previously after George's death. George never gave up on him either: in later years, long after they had gone their separate ways, he would invite Andrew to join him on stage, invitations that were always refused as Andrew continued to keep the past firmly in the past, rarely emerging from his self-imposed exile from Planet Showbiz. Ironically, George ended up envying his old friend, who was able to create a contented personal life away from the limelight.

When the two twelve-year-olds met it became apparent just how well Jack Panos had done for himself and also how much the boys had in common. "What surprised me was how wealthy they were," Andrew later recalled in an interview with the *Daily Mirror*. "Later I realized that his mum and dad had started out on an economical class level that was very similar to my parents. Like my father, his father was an immigrant [as said, Andrew is of Egyptian-Italian stock] and they both married these very, very English girls and I suppose the girls took a risk when they married the foreigners."

The youngsters quickly became inseparable. Another of George's problems that dated from childhood was dissatisfaction with his appearance: as a young teen he was plump from comfort eating, suffered acne and wore thick glasses. "I was a very unattractive adolescent," he said in 1987. "I had glasses and… you know, spots. I don't see that person in the mirror any more, but I know that deep inside I'm still making up for the fat kid."

The close friendship between the two boys lightly alarmed George's parents. Worse still, it emerged that Andrew also wanted to be a pop star, which meant that there were now two of them absolutely set on a career that George's father, Jack, at least, was horrified by. "There was always a bit of a tense air when I went round there," said Andrew in a lengthy profile of George that appeared in *Rolling Stone* magazine after he went solo in 1986.

But George was to recall that meeting Andrew would prove the making of him. "In retrospect I've never seen two people that were so influential on each other's lives and characters," he admitted in an interview with *Rolling Stone* in 1988. "Andrew and I, in a sense, totally changed each other. I suppose we spent all that time aspiring to be different parts of each other. I mean, we would go out and get absolutely wrecked at that age—14, 15, 16—when you go to parties and all you want to do is get off with someone. And in the course of that pursuit you get absolutely legless. The majority of the time Andrew got more legless than I, so I'd have to carry him home. I remember evenings when he'd be fallin' over and throwin' up, and I'd sit him in his front room, and his clothes would be immaculate. And I'd be absolutely covered in shit, you know? His clothes were always perfect, he was really stylish, all the girls liked him. And that was something that I always wanted to be, because I was such a mess to look at. The whole idea of being a physically attractive personality never really occurred to me until I met him."

Andrew agreed with this description. "He didn't have much of a clue about making the most of himself then," he told *Rolling Stone*. "George probably wanted to be rich and famous—most of us do, I think—but I don't think he ever wanted to be a star. But George was incredibly consumed by music, and I think it was my desire to entertain and his desire to write songs that really brought the whole thing together."

And so while Andrew watched out for him at school, George's sisters took charge at home. The glasses were swapped for contact lenses, specialist creams saw to the acne, eyebrows were plucked and a perm sorted his hair out. George Michael the future pop star was beginning to emerge. Andrew, much the sharper dresser of the two, began to encourage his new friend to wear slightly more fashionable clothes. And their love of pop music was drawing them ever closer. As they chatted and played their music together—an early favorite being Elton John's "Goodbye Yellow Brick Road"—to their mutual delight they discovered they wanted exactly the same thing—to be pop stars. But then an awful lot of teenagers share that same ambition. It was not quite obvious at this early stage that they were to become members of the rare breed who would make it from the daydream stage to glorious reality.

The young George did have a few girlfriends but, as with most gay men, he had been aware that he was gay from an early age; although, according to him, in his earliest years he thought he was straight and then went through a long patch of believing that he was bisexual, as he told Andrew Ridgeley and other friends when he was nineteen. One of the reasons he took a long time to come out was his mother: it was widely assumed that George protected her as this was the era when AIDS was taking its dreadful toll, and so he didn't want to tell her the truth. However, while that is part of it, there was another element as well: Lesley's brother Colin was thought to be gay and in that very different pre-gay-rights time ended up committing suicide, as did his maternal grandfather. (George eventually paid tribute to his late uncle with the song "My Mother Had A Brother.") But that meant alongside all the other tensions and unspoken fears in the family, there were two recent suicides, one of them involving a gay man, and an unspoken fear that it would happen again. Small wonder George had such a problem coming out.

Years later, in 2007, George told the *Mirror*: "My mother had this fear of me being gay. She had this definite fear that I was going to be like her brother—she thought that it meant I wouldn't cope with life. She almost felt like she had brought this gene. So there were very pointed areas where she let my dad be—supposedly protectively—homophobic. There was this gay waiter who lived above our family restaurant and I wasn't allowed to go to the top flat when he was in the restaurant. You know, in case I caught something. In case I caught gay. Knowing my father, he couldn't even consider he had a gay son because he is of his generation, a Greek Cypriot man.

"But my mother was afraid of my father's judgment of me. I also now realize she was afraid that if the 'gene' was in me it would turn out the same way for me as it had for Colin. My mother didn't talk about her brother until I was 16. I don't know if that was a decision on her part or whether she just plucked up the courage. It changed my opinion of her entirely because it wasn't just that—she's also seen her own father die the same way. They'd both put their heads in the gas oven. And lucky old Mum, she found both of them. She spent years being so remorseful that it's impossible to hold that time against her. And in the last 20 years of her life, I don't think we had a cross word actually."

However, unlike many gay men George ascribes his homosexuality to nurture, not nature, on the grounds that his father was absent so much during his childhood that he grew closer to women and began to identify with them instead. In a somewhat eye-watering 2004 interview with *GQ* magazine—the older George did not worry about shocking people—he expanded on this theme: "In my case it was a nurture thing, via the absence of my father who was always busy working," he explained.

"It meant I was exceptionally close to my mother. All of my early sexual fantasies were straight and totally readable... It wasn't until puberty that I started fantasising about men, and I do think it had something to do with my environment. But there are definitely those who have a predisposition to being gay in which the environment is irrelevant."

But it was not a universally held view among the gay community and in that particular interview George also raised eyebrows by saying that if he hadn't been with his then boyfriend, Kenny Goss, he might have been with a woman. In retrospect, this simply comes across as deeply conflicted. Even though George finally came out in 1998 and even made jokes about being caught in public lavatories (he was arrested by an undercover officer in a Beverly Hills park in 1988 after being caught in a "lewd act" in a public lavatory), it still appears that he maintained an ambiguous relationship with his own sexuality, another reason why he found it so difficult to achieve peace.

And there was still the issue with his mother who, he worried in that same interview, didn't see him as man enough when he was growing up. Clearly, the issue with his uncle had, understandably, struck a deep chord and George himself was entirely understanding about why Lesley had been so concerned. "She was so liberal as a parent that it didn't make sense that she might feel like that," he explained to *GQ*. "But I think it was because her brother Colin had killed himself the day after I was born, and she thought it was because he was gay. So I'm sure she was terrified of seeing anything gay about me because, to her, being gay meant misery. I totally understand that, even though she was misguided in worrying about it."

Andrew Ridgeley was actually one of the first people in whom George would confide, once the heady days of Wham! began. However, at that stage George still thought he might be bisexual, and he did go on to have relationships with women, of which more anon.

As the two boys grew up, both became increasingly obsessed with music and George began to bring something to the party of his own. Andrew had initially been the dominant partner in the friendship, but that began to change slightly as George had an extensive knowledge of pop music and soon it was pretty obvious that he was talented as well. He was fast growing out of his puppy fat and into his looks too. The pair would often go into central London to busk on the Underground: they would take their musical choices from the recently released Queen album, *A Night At The Opera* (1975), specifically the track "39," which many years later George would sing at the Freddie Mercury Tribute Concert at Wembley Stadium in April 1992. George also began work as a DJ, finding gigs at local schools and clubs in Watford, Bushey and Stanmore, as well as taking on other temporary roles to support himself when needed, such as a cinema usher and working on a building site. Jack Panos, who hadn't spent his life bettering himself and his family to see his son embark on a useless quest to become a musician, was not amused.

Lesley was far more positive, however, and encouraged her boy to follow his dream. "She pretty much used to go along with my dad in that she wanted me to get an education so that if this incredible dream I had didn't work out, I would have something to fall back on," George told *Interview* magazine in 1988. "But she's much more musical, and by the time I started writing songs—by the time I was about 17—she started to believe in me, musically." But that was when problems with his father really began to develop: concerned that the young George would be going nowhere, at one point Jack told his son to get a recording contract within six months or get out of the house.

In later years George was to credit teenage clashes with his father with turning him into the entertainer he became. "But you know, a lot of people with a childhood like that turn it to their advantage," he told the *Huffington Post* in 2009. "The fact I had my father as an adversary was such a powerful tool to work with. I subconsciously fought him to the degree that [it] drove me to be one of the most successful musicians in the world."

However, at the time it was difficult. Some of George's more bitter remarks in later life stem from this period: a father who didn't think he could sing and thought he wouldn't hack it in the admittedly tough music business. On the one side there was Andrew Ridgeley and a group of other friends as well as his mother encouraging him to give it a go; on the other the sternly patriarchal figure of the Greek Cypriot father, wanting his only son to get a good job. In the end, of course, George followed his dream and made it, spectacularly, far faster than anyone would have thought possible, and after that spent his relatively short life at the pinnacle of his profession. He also went on to establish a very good relationship with his father, who was always there for him during his various health crises and was to become extremely proud of his talented boy. And so, George and Andrew started making proper plans for the future: they decided to form a band.

# 3

# WHAM, BAM, I AM A MAN

The year 1979 was to herald an era of intense cultural change. The Conservative Party were elected under their first-ever female leader Margaret Thatcher and she and her fellow Tories were to sweep away the old order and establish a more brassy era, one in which George Michael and Andrew Ridgeley, despite having very different political convictions, were to flourish. 1979 was also the year in which the two boys decided to take their music seriously and, whatever reservations George's father had, make a go of it.

It was in the summer, after exams, that the new venture started to take shape. George and Andrew, along with Andrew's brother Paul, David Austin and Andrew Leaver (who shared a birthday with the other Andrew and tragically died of cancer at twenty) put together a ska 2-tone outfit they called The Executive. They rehearsed in various family sitting rooms and George's stage debut actually took place on November 5, 1979 in a Methodist church hall in Bushey, Hertfordshire. Though attended mainly by the boys' friends and family, it was on the whole deemed to be a success.

One person was yet to be convinced, however: Jack Panos. "Me and my dad were having this big argument," George would later recall. "We were driving in the car and I was playing him this demo tape. Apart from 'Rude Boy' [the band's theme tune] I had done something with David [Austin] and I was plugging this thing around all the record companies as well. And I remember playing it in the car to my dad and he was going on about how I had to realize that there was no future in this for me. He had been telling me all this for years and I had given up arguing with him long ago—I knew he wouldn't take any notice. But now I really had a go at him. I said, you have been rubbing this shit into my face for the last five years. I told him, there is no way I am not going to try to do this so the least you could do is give me some moral support. 'All 17-year-olds want to be pop stars,' he said. 'No, Dad,' I said. 'All 12-year-olds want to be pop stars.'" (Quoted in George Michael's 1991 autobiography, *Bare*, co-written with Tony Parsons.)

And this was to be the trial run before the Wham! madness set in and in later years Andrew rather modestly commented that, "Getting George into a band at 16 was one of my most important contributions." George was still at school, studying English Literature and Art—he had given up on Musical Theory, funnily enough—while Andrew had already left and had gone on to Cassio College, a sixth-form college in Watford.

The Executive continued its short-lived existence, although Andrew Leaver left soon afterwards, but they got as far as cutting a demo tape, which featured "Rude Boy," a ska cover of the Andy Williams' hit "Can't Get Used To Losing You" and, a real rarity, a ska version of Beethoven's piano solo "Für Elise." George and Andrew started taking the short journey into central London to play the demo tape to the A&R men at various record companies, but didn't get very far. Andrew put it down to them being too old to appreciate the music; George wondered if the track wasn't good enough and told himself firmly that he must do better next time.

It is thought that there were never more than ten copies of the demo tape made and all have disappeared. It is also believed that the boys added more tracks to the later tapes, ending up with between six and eight, and it is further rumored that one of those additional tracks was an early version of "Careless Whisper," certainly not a ska number. It was a short clip, lasting just twenty seconds, and there was also the beginning of what would become "Wham Rap!." But it seems unlikely that the demo will ever be found. The group continued to tour in local venues, including Cassio College, when a sudden spat caused them to split. A gig at Harrow College had supposedly been arranged, supporting punk band The Vibrators, but when George and Andrew looked into it more closely, they found that nothing had been set up. The group broke up with some acrimony: Paul went off to play in a jazz band, David went to the Far East and George and Andrew briefly tried to work with an older crowd of musicians, but the two young men just couldn't fit in with them. And so George and Andrew decided they would have a shot at making it on their own.

But now, as a duo, the boys needed another demo. The Ridgeley front room was commandeered for a rented porta-studio, for which the two paid £20, and here they recorded "Wham Rap!," "Club Tropicana," "Come On!" and "Careless Whisper." Although both worked on all four tracks, it is remarkable to think that the two of them penned these future huge hits when they were still about seventeen. That last song, in particular, seems to denote an emotional maturity well beyond their years and it should be noted here that Andrew Ridgeley was the co-writer. Most of the band's later songs were written solely by George, but the smash hit "Careless Whisper" is listed as a joint creation. In later years, people would say that George gave Andrew a co-writing credit as a sort of gift-cum-pension in the form of future royalties, but if that is true it showed remarkable prescience on his part given the song was written before they had so much as released a single, let alone experienced the kind of success that was to come their way. What is undoubtedly true, though, is that it is one of the reasons that Andrew was able to retire from the music business before he was thirty and live in comfort from then on.

Another round of approaches to record labels followed along with another round of rejections. "Get yourself a job," said Jack Panos. George ignored him. "Or get out of this house," Jack continued, or at least used words to that effect in his exasperation that his only son still wanted to be a pop star. Again George chose to ignore his father's advice. Then someone heard the tape after bumping into the pair at the Three Crowns pub in Bushey and realized that these were not just another going-nowhere couple of pop wannabes. That person was Mark Dean, who worked in the record business and who also knew the Ridgeley family. He had already discovered Soft Cell and ABC. He was about to hit the jackpot once more. "The person who discovered him [George] was my mother," said Dean somewhat self-deprecatingly in later years, but at the time he signed the boys up to a deal that George was later to spend years complaining about, with the label Innervision, a subsidiary of CBS. Their first manager was Bryan Morrison and they were getting ready to make quite an impact on the world.

In the meantime the boys had been honing their dance skills. Andrew's then girlfriend was Shirlie Holliman, a singer and dancer who appeared with Wham! as a backing singer and later became half of the pop duo Pepsie & Shirlie. The three of them would go out on the town, dancing at clubs such as Le Beat Route in Soho and funking it up to the music of the era, by bands such as Earth, Wind & Fire, the Bee Gees and Chic. "It was so much fun," Shirlie told *Classic Pop* in March 2015. "The three of us got on brilliantly—they became my world. We'd all go dancing together and Wham! started out as an extension of that. They were great times but I sometimes felt like a spare part next to George—his talent overawed me, and still does. He was the organizer and Andrew had the charisma."

The trio were then joined by a fourth singer and dancer, Dee C. Lee: "I was working as an in-house session singer at EMI Publishing, recording maybe three or four tracks a day for the songwriters signed," she told *Classic Pop*. "Someone from Innervision contacted EMI about a new boyband that wanted two female singers—one black and one white. I met them and we just clicked. They were really young and innocent, very sweet and great fun. Recording 'Fantastic' was great—although I'd worked in studios before, this was a new experience for us all and so exciting. George particularly had driving passion and ambition—and, of course, the songs were brilliant. I knew they were going to be huge."

Shirlie and Dee were never actually part of Wham! per se, occupying the roles of dancers and backing singers, but they certainly contributed to the band's early success.

The boys recorded their four demo tracks professionally, plus a fifth one "Young Guns (Go For It!)" written by George alone. It was then decided that "Wham Rap!" would be the boys' debut single: it was an extremely uptempo number about having fun even when unemployed ("You're gonna have a good time down on the line") and the frequent references to parents constantly telling their young son to find himself a decent job must have originated from George's ongoing run-ins with his father. The initial release was a double A-side with a "Social Mix" and an "Anti-Social Mix," which proved to be counterproductive as the BBC refused to put it on the playlist because of the bad language used in the "Anti-Social Mix." Two videos were made to go with each but only one, the famous version, is remembered now.

Unemployment in the UK was in fact running high at the time and this was putting a positive spin on what was a much worried-about social phenomenon of the day. The two boys and their backing singers embarked on a tour of the clubs, performing the song live, which was to prove invaluable experience for the future, even if it wasn't too much fun at the time. "Those PAs were the best practice in the world," George recalled to *Classic Pop* in March 2015. "They were awful and amateur but we had to do them; there was no way we could make those dance routines up in my mum's living room and expect them to translate straight away onto live television."

Dee remembered them as well: "Those club tours were extremely hard work—sometimes, five or six shows a night —but we enjoyed all of it," she told *Classic Pop*. "As it was a new and fresh experience, it didn't really feel like work. We were always surprised by the fantastic reaction from the audiences, and became more confident with every show."

In June 1982, "Wham Rap!" was released as a single

and although now considered a classic, at the time it went nowhere fast, stalling at No. 105 in the UK charts. The accompanying video makes interesting viewing: it shows George prancing about in black leather (looking, with the benefit of hindsight, not entirely heterosexual), before dancing into Andrew's house, where his friend's parents are nagging him to get a job, getting him to dump the cardigan he has been wearing, giving him cooler clothes to wear and dragging him out of the house. In reality, of course, it had been entirely the other way round: it was Andrew who turned George into the streetwise young man he had become. The two of them end up, leather-clad, dancing with the girls.

What is notable about the video is that there is no question that George was in charge. When the two first became friends, Andrew was the dominant partner, now George was patently running the show. It is George who is lively, George who opens a window of escape, and George, who, fizzing with energy, can barely contain himself. In contrast, Andrew appears laid-back, languid even, and in many ways this video foreshadowed what was to come, because it was Andrew who chose the more relaxed approach to life in the longer term. However, it cannot be stressed enough that for all that it was George who had the major musical talent, Wham! could not have existed without Andrew Ridgeley. He did far more than just persuade George to join the band. Simon Napier-Bell, who managed the band from 1983–86 and who had also overseen the fortunes of Japan and Marc Bolan, told *Classic Pop* in the same article from March 2015, "Andrew was the image. Wham! was two lads around town—heterosexual and having fun. George invented the image of the band from observing Andrew. He then chose to act out the role of the second of the two lads around town. Sure, George wrote the songs, but songwriters can be hired or recruited—the one essential of any group is its personality, its image. And that was pure Andrew. Without him, Wham! could never have existed."

Initially, it seemed that George's father had been proven right, but in actual fact the boys were not going to have to wait long for their big break. It happened almost immediately. They were still going strong in the clubs and it was while performing "Young Guns (Go For It!)" in the famous Stringfellows nightclub, which had just been released as their second single and which seemed destined to hover forever on the outer reaches of the charts, that they were spotted by someone at the BBC. This led to an invitation to appear on *Saturday Superstore*; the single started to rise up the charts and, shortly afterwards, for the first time ever, the boys started to become aware that they were being recognized. Wham! was on its way.

"Young Guns" is another song and video that bears re-examination. "Well, I haven't seen your face around town awhile," a leather-jacketed George sings on spotting a tie-wearing Andrew in a nightclub, before going on to establish that Andrew is engaged and warning him of the dire consequences of getting married: "A married man?

You're out of your head ... ," sings George, before adding, in case the point has been lost, "Death by matrimony!"

In the video, Andrew ends up shoving his girlfriend in a manner that would probably see him arrested today before disappearing off with his friend to have fun, but again, with hindsight, it is hard not to suspect that George's real point might have been a little different from the way it came across at the time. It was presented as two young bucks gallivanting around and being far too young to settle down, but, actually, George was warning his friend away from having a relationship with a woman. Make of that what you will. And again, in the video, George comes across as by far the more dominant partner: it is he who butts into Andrew's life as Andrew looks on with a positively resigned expression. Could it have been that even as far back as 1982, Andrew was becoming increasingly aware that this wasn't exactly what he wanted? Certainly from watching the video, with no prior knowledge of the duo, you would never have guessed that Ridgeley had once been the one who set everything in motion.

The boys appeared on the BBC's *Top Of The Pops*, with George sporting espadrilles, a suede jacket and rolled-up jeans. Andrew stood behind him with the girls. The audience, specifically young, teenage girls, went wild. The song got to No. 3 in the UK charts. "Wham Rap!" was immediately re-released and this time went to No. 8, the second of four hits from Wham!'s debut album, *Fantastic*. A tour—the Club Fantastic '83 Tour—followed, as the UK fell under the spell of these exuberant boys from North London; they even had their own warm-up act, "knobbly-kneed MC" Capital Radio DJ Gary Crowley—remarkable when you consider that just a year earlier they had themselves been preparing to be a warm-up act for The Vibrators. Another single quickly followed, "Bad Boys," which got to No. 2, although George always professed himself very unhappy with the song. "I wrote to a formula for 'Bad Boys,' trying to replicate something else," he told *Classic Pop*. "That's something I'd never done before and have never done since."

Because the substance of the earliest singles focused on actual social problems—unemployment, the foolishness of getting hitched too young—Wham! briefly gained a reputation as a dance protest group, but that didn't last long, especially after the release of "Club Tropicana," of which more below. And now the boys became aware of another problem: they had been so keen to sign with a record label that they hadn't realized the terms were not favorable to them. At this stage, although they had made a huge splash and had pitched headfirst into fame, they suddenly became aware that they were expected to live on a measly £40-a-week allowance from Innervision.

Not for the last time, George sought to extricate himself from a record contract. Simon and Jazz Summers had set up Nomis Management and in 1983 the boys turned to them for help: "I was confident that we could get them out of it," Simon told *Classic Pop*. "Contracts as bad as that can't stand up in British courts. But it wasn't easy—for one thing, money was needed to fight it and they didn't have any. And secondly, we were up against CBS, who had more money than any other record company in the world."

These issues aside, the boys were on a roll. It had become obvious where their strengths lay and so George concentrated on the composing and singing aspect of the business while Andrew set the tone for the style and image of the band. Next up was "Club Tropicana," a slight change of emphasis in that the leather jackets were cast aside and the "baby biker" image replaced with something that wouldn't have looked out of place in a Duran Duran video. It was a pleasant enough little melody about two handsome young men taking a Club 18–30-style holiday; or at any rate a *satire* of two handsome young men taking a Club 18–30 style holiday, depending on who you spoke to. Whether the intent was satirical or not, it certainly tapped into the spirit of the time: mass tourism was becoming the norm and vast numbers flew out every year to exactly the same kind of resort the two boys were cavorting around in. And it all served to polish the image of two playboys out to have fun; heterosexual fun, of course. George's secret was still very secret indeed.

The video was filmed at Pikes Hotel in Ibiza and set up as a film starring George and Andrew (George got top billing); there were jolly scenes of George drinking cocktails, both of them having showers; both playing trumpets before falling backwards into the swimming pool. Shirlie Holliman and

Dee C. Lee were also there, exchanging pouting looks with the boys until, in a final twist, if you can call it that, it is revealed that George and Andrew are pilots and the girls are air stewardesses.

The song became the fourth hit from the album *Fantastic* and got to No. 4 in the UK charts. Dee left soon afterwards to work with Paul Weller and the Style Council and was replaced by Pepsi DeMacque (who would later, post-Wham!, team up with Shirlie Holliman to form Pepsi & Shirlie).

In 1986, around the time Wham! broke up, George gave a revealing interview to *NME*, reflecting on their success and observing, accurately, that Wham! had in some ways been a personification of that particular time in the 1980s when society was turning on its head. There were not many in the artistic community who would stand up for Margaret Thatcher but, although he was certainly never an actual supporter of the Iron Lady, George sometimes sounded suspiciously sympathetic to what was going on.

"Basically, the whole American ideal of the possibility of becoming middle-class, the idea of aspiration, was something that was going to happen," he explained in an interview with *NME* in 1986. "The idea of the '80s being sex and suntans, and us being the epitome of it is perfectly true. We're up there, supposedly promoting it, but it's there anyway. Kids have now decided that when they're 13 and 14 they don't want to be teenagers, they don't want the next seven years to be a time when they go out and experiment and totally disassociate themselves with childhood and adulthood, which is basically what I grew up with. I did the soulboy bit and went through a Mod period as well: I didn't want to look like my parents or the way I'd looked a couple of years before. Glamor is seen in this country as America. We just picked up on the normal traits of stardom, and as my musical angle has always had an American side, the two things fitted. England suddenly became like *Miami Vice* in the rain, and that combined with the quality of what we were doing. It all fitted together very nicely, though I didn't plan it that way."

He was also, however, aware of a certain polarisation within the UK, the fact that there was a growing divide between North and South. "You've always got to remember you're talking from a London and South East point of view," he continued in the same *NME* interview. "The North doesn't look like this. Most of them don't have the time or money to even pretend. But for most teenagers London has not become a poor place to live. London has benefited from the whole right-wing idea. I don't honestly think that the people that are going to these wine bars and souping up Escorts feel that things are getting worse. They're not the people on the dole; they're the people that have got a few bob to fritter away. I used to believe that people were taking on these Americanisms as a form of escape from what was really going on. I don't think that applies any more. I don't think that those people have got the things to escape from, they're not the people face-to-face with the real problems. But it's very hard for me to sit here and judge that now; I can only guess."

In the video for "Club Tropicana," the two boys, with their olive skin, white teeth and coiffed and highlighted hair, look impossibly handsome, the very epitome of the glamor George had been talking about. Almost certainly they would have fitted straight in to *Miami Vice*. They had become bona fide heartthrobs, with teenage fans arguing as to which was the more desirable. Teen magazines were putting them on the cover and printing posters of them; details about their backgrounds were beginning to emerge —the friendship that had started at school, their likes and dislikes. During the course of their tour they became notorious for stuffing shuttlecocks down their shorts, reducing fans to screaming wrecks. "The tour was chaos," Shirlie told *Classic Pop* in March 2015, "all these screaming fans wanting to get in with George and Andrew. They'd ask Pepsi and I to pass on messages for them with their phone numbers and underwear attached. But it didn't work."

Going through the girls may not have worked but every pop star since the genre was invented has found him or herself to be the center of attention from groupies and George and Andrew were no different. At this stage no one outside George's innermost circle had a clue he might be gay; even there the real status quo was not entirely clear. George had confided in Andrew that he might be bisexual, but he himself later went on record—for instance, in an interview with *GQ* in 2004—to talk about his belief that it was nurture, not nature, that had made him gay and at such a young age, with so many attractive women throwing themselves at him, it was hardly surprising if he felt a little confused. And so, with so many offers on the table, he accepted many of them at the time.

"I used to sleep with women quite a lot in the Wham! days but never felt it could develop into a relationship because I knew that, emotionally, I was a gay man," he told *GQ* many years later, in the 2004 interview mentioned above. "I didn't want to commit to them but I was attracted to them. Then I became ashamed that I might be using them. I decided I had to stop, which I did when I began to worry about AIDS, which was becoming prevalent in Britain. Although I had always had safe sex, I didn't want to sleep with a woman without telling her I was bisexual. I felt that would be irresponsible. Basically, I didn't want to have that uncomfortable conversation that might ruin the moment, so I stopped sleeping with them."

But it was a complex area and George did go on to have one girlfriend, of which more anon. Again in the same interview in 2004, he also confessed to *GQ* to fancying one of the other great pop icons of the era who, like George, endured: Madonna "during her chubby years... I felt she was really trying to suss out whether I would go for it or not. But I was only 23 and was really intimidated because I felt like she was coming onto me and although I thought that she was sexy, she was just too powerful for me at that stage. She's very strong. Her sexuality is hers, it's not for men, and I had a feeling it would be sex of an intensity that would feel like I was with a man. I don't know why. Maybe I should have tried it!"

None of this was even hinted at in public back then. George and Andrew were handsome and virile young men and, as far as everyone was concerned, very heterosexual indeed, which in the case of Andrew was actually true. George said in later years that he had been upset when their manager talked about the fact that Wham! was the real Andrew and the fake Andrew—namely George—but there was a certain amount of truth to it. Andrew really was a confident, sunny and laid-back man about town; George, as became so painfully clear in subsequent years, was not. But there was no question of his coming out at that point —it would have destroyed Wham!—and so, just twenty, he found himself weighed down with an enormous secret that he would not be able to go public with for many years.

That said, at the time the two young men had achieved all they wanted and more. George's father Jack was wrong: his son had what it took to be a major star and everyone in the family was thrilled. The boys also eventually succeeded in getting out of their contract with Innervision, which had in the interim released a medley of tracks from the album *Fantastic* that had not been released as singles and called it the *Club Fantastic Megamix*. The boys urged the public *not* to buy it. They were in a fight with Innervision and wanted control over the material they had worked so hard to create.

But, now that they were free, they were able to start on a second album, *Make It Big*, which in turn would develop their image further from plasticky pop stars to something with a great deal more substance. It was also becoming increasingly obvious which of the two would probably have the longer-term future in the industry, although the older George also lamented that because his own career eventually became so high profile, Andrew was very unfairly overlooked. But back then so ubiquitous had the band become in such a short space of time that it sometimes appeared as if they had sprung, fully formed, from nowhere. And it wasn't just in the UK, either: their singles were charting across the globe and quite soon they would be touring far beyond the UK as well. Within the space of less than a year, George and Andrew had turned into two of the biggest stars in the world.

# 4

# GUILTY FEET
# HAVE GOT
# NO RHYTHM

By the time the boys got to work on their second album, *Make It Big*, George's attitude to his growing fame was becoming increasingly ambivalent. On the one hand it was beginning to get on his nerves and in order to try to escape some of the attention, the recording was done in Studio Miraval, southern France, where he also consolidated his hold over his output by working as sole producer, a position he maintained until Wham! split up in 1986. On the other hand, he rather enjoyed it.

George was absolutely in his prime: he was looking as good as he was ever going to look and he cultivated his image, appearing done up to the nines whenever he left the house, be it for professional or personal reasons. It was remarked upon that he complained about the attention he would get when, say, walking through an airport, but that he encouraged this attention as much as anyone given his proclivity to appear in leather jackets rather than, say, a novercoat. It was an ambivalence that was to grow, not least because he had still not come to terms with his sexuality.

To the outside world, at least, there was no indication of any inner torment: indeed, all anyone saw was that even greater acclaim was coming the boys' way. The new album was a huge success, although it was becoming increasingly obvious that George was the driving force behind it while Andrew really had taken second place. Christopher Connelly from *Rolling Stone* said, "George Michael's music is an unabashed rehash of Motown"and "*Make It Big* [is an] almost flawless pop record, a record that does exactly what it wants to and has a great deal of fun doing it." Stephen Thomas Erlewine of AllMusic opined, "They succeeded on a grander scale than they ever could have imagined, conquering the world and elsewhere with this effervescent set of giddy new wave pop-soul, thereby making George Michael a superstar and consigning Andrew Ridgeley to the confines of Trivial Pursuit." If Andrew minded this somewhat harsh judgement (and you would have had to have had a pretty thick skin not to be affected), he said nothing in public and, like the pro he was, simply got on with the show.

*Make It Big* contains some of the band's best-known songs: "Wake Me Up Before You Go-Go," "Everything She Wants," "Freedom" and, of course, the ballad "Careless Whisper," with its co-credit to Andrew Ridgeley. George himself remained firm that it was a co-creation: he later told *Rolling Stone* that Andrew came up with the chord patterns and also some of the lyrics. Critics at the time could not have known that it had actually been written a couple of years earlier, which may be why the story about George gifting half the songwriting royalties to Andrew began, but it was to be just one of a number of resounding successes at the time. "Wake Me Up" got the boys to Number 1 in the UK and the US for the first time, while "Careless Whisper," released as a solo by George, reached Number 1 in twenty-five countries around the world, the UK and US included. "Freedom" (not to be confused with "Freedom! '90") also became a UK Number 1. The band were by now indisputably one of the biggest acts in the world.

"In late 1983 or early 1984, after I'd gone freelance and engineered the Alarm's *Declaration* with producer Alan Shacklock, I got a call from Wham!'s then-manager Jazz Summers, asking if I'd work with them on their next album, *Make It Big*," George's long-time sound engineer Chris Porter told *Sound on Sound* in March 2013, providing a fascinating insight into the way George worked. "For me, that was a fantastic opportunity. The first track we did was 'Wake Me Up Before You Go-Go,' recorded within a couple of days at Sarm West's Studio 2. Although there wasn't a demo, George had most of the song written in his head and we recorded it with a live band. Then, for the next track, 'Careless Whisper,' George and Andrew went to Muscle Shoals [in Alabama] to work with producer Jerry

Wexler and I thought, 'That's it. My involvement with Wham! is over. There's no way I'm ever going to see them again.'" That version of the song nearly ended up on the *Club Fantastic Megamix*, but legal action prevented it.

Porter took up the story again. "A few weeks later, I got a call telling me George wasn't happy with 'Careless Whisper' and wanted to know if I'd help him re-record it," he told *Sound On Sound*. "Of course I could, so we went back into Studio 2 at Sarm and worked on that track with a live rhythm section. It took quite a long time to make and we went through 11 sax players to find one who could get the solo's main phrase done in one breath."

The sax solo of course, played by Steve Gregory, was to become as famous as the sax solo on Gerry Rafferty's "Baker Street" (1978), while the video, filmed in Miami, consolidated George's position as a major heartthrob, all longing intensity as he reflects on his guilt at cheating on his girlfriend, played by model Lisa Stahl. It was a song that not only sold in the millions but went far beyond its creators' initial hopes and expectations, covered by many other singers since then and largely accepted as a classic.

It is odd then that George himself was extremely dismissive: "[It] was not an integral part of my emotional development," he said in his 1991 autobiography, *Bare*. "It disappoints me that you can write a lyric very flippantly – and not a particularly good lyric—and it can mean so much to so many people. That's disillusioning for a writer." It was pretty disillusioning for the millions of punters who bought it, too, but then again George may well have been conflicted that "Careless Whisper" effectively turned him into the leading heterosexual sex symbol of the day, a role he took many years and a great deal of effort attempting to shed. With the benefit of hindsight, it's hardly surprising that all those inner torments became so self-destructive.

Indeed, George's attitude towards much of his Wham! output fluctuated but, as he grew older, he seemed to relax far more about songs he wrote at the beginning of his career and despite the fact that "Careless Whisper" is probably the best known of them all, he never really acknowledged it as a great song. "I'm still a bit puzzled why it's made such an impression on people," he told *Rolling Stone* in 2009. "Is it because so many people have cheated on their partners? Is that why they connect with it? I have no idea, but it's ironic that this song—which has come to define me in some way —should have been written right at the beginning of my career when I was still so young. I was only 17 and didn't really know much about anything—and certainly nothing much about relationships."

It was also the first real indication that George's future lay as a solo artist and not with Andrew Ridgeley. Others were noticing it too. "By the time of *Make It Big*, Andrew's musical involvement was pretty much non-existent—he was more of an emotional pillar than a musical presence," Chris Porter told *Sound On Sound* in March 2013. "Meanwhile, George and I always had a really, really good working relationship. Although he's 10 years younger than me, I had a tremendous respect for his ability, his musicality and his drive. He was an exceptionally driven man and had a really clear idea about what he wanted to achieve. It was my first experience of interacting with someone who had songs— and the sounds of those songs—in his head. He'd come to the studio knowing what he wanted to accomplish. That album was really our impression of Motown, and although it sometimes perhaps didn't achieve the sonic quality, it kind of achieved the spirit and liveliness of those records."

But working with people with whom he did not share the same emotional connection as he did with Andrew Ridgeley was to be of scant comfort in the years ahead. Whatever Andrew's musical contribution, the fact is that the two of them had known one another since they were twelve years old and he provided a form of emotional stability for George that no one else would ever be able to do. The two of them were at the center of that whirlwind together: no one outside the partnership could really understand what it was like to go from the undistinguished suburbs of London to the heights of international pop stardom in such a short space of time. And George could confide in Andrew: he was one of the few people who knew about the issues with his friend's sexuality. George was to keep his life on an even keel for more than another decade, but it is hard not to come to the conclusion that as he and Andrew began to edge in different directions, he lost a lifeline that had kept him stable for years.

Although they kept going for another two years, the

seeming inequality between the pair became increasingly clear. Andrew was keenly aware that his partner had a unique talent. "George felt under a bit of pressure coming up with material, and I said to Andrew, 'Can't you help him write these things?'," Jazz Summers later told *Rolling Stone* in 1986. "And he said, 'If I write a song, I might write a brilliant song. But George Michael will write an even more brilliant one. The bloke's a fucking genius. It's pointless for me to write a song.' Andrew was just being very pragmatic about it."

George himself was beginning to realize what was happening. "The first year, when Andrew and I realized things had to change, there was friction," he told *Rolling Stone* shortly after thesplit in 1986. "We'd start getting rude with each other. There was a time I was really pissed off at him, because he'd been late for a photo or recording session. I was saying, 'For fuck's sake, I'm doing all the work on this album. The least you can do is take care of your side of things.' We argued about it, and when I argue, I force the truth from people. And what he was feeling was he couldn't bear the unspoken un-evenness of it. Once it was out in the open, neither of us had any problem with it."

In truth, Andrew was in an extremely difficult position, but until the split there wasn't a great deal he could do. He started to develop an interest in motor racing, a safer ground—he wouldn't be expected to compete with George there.

Over a decade later, George was adopting a very different tone when looking back on this period of his life. He had been young and carefree and astoundingly successful and all the complaints about press intrusion or the meaninglessness of "Careless Whisper" were gone. "I see now that my time with Wham! were the happiest years of my life," he told the *Mirror* when he was thirty-four, in an interview with Tony Parsons published in November 1997. "When I listen to our records I hear two young men who are having the best time they would ever have. It's amazing—the joy in it, the spirit of it. I listen to myself singing in Wham! and I think —who is that person? And I know who he is, and I know who those two boys are—two kids at the top of a dream…

"I can see now that you have this fantastic period in the middle of your life between living with your parents and settling down when, probably for the purpose of making sure you go out shagging and procreate, you can briefly be your own creation. That was Wham! for me. Wham! were shamelessly joyful. I knew I wasn't cred—but I didn't know how to be cred. I had no idea what to wear. I had no real idea about adult sex. I was just a kid with a smart musical head. I couldn't try to be cool. I didn't know how. So Andrew and I just had a laugh. I was smart musically but at the same time there was a certain childishness about it all – and that's what made the records so good. There were about 18 months when it was pure joy—the realisation of dreams. All these things that I had dreamed about, like having a lot of probably quite useless sex. I was 20 years old and my dreams were coming true. There's a window in there where I was blissfully happy." Sadly, it did not last for long.

Nor, it seemed, did Andrew have the same gilded view of the past as George, not least because he became so comprehensively overshadowed despite the fact that the band had started out as very much a joint venture. "Andrew was my best mate from the age of 12 until just before the end of the group," George told the *Mirror* in the same interview, years after Wham! broke up. "To be honest, Andrew's relationship to the past is different from mine. He has taken a severe beating from the press because my career has stayed so high profile. I'm not saying he blames me in any way but it has pushed him away from the past.

"He wants nothing more to do with the music industry. He doesn't want to hear about it. He doesn't want to talk about it. And it's my life. There's no strain or rift between us but we don't see each other because he lives in Cornwall and he wants to move on. But I feel more affection for Wham! as time goes by."

In fact, they did keep in touch and Andrew was sufficiently generous in spirit to say, after George's death, that George should not just be referred to as a member of Wham! because he had achieved so much more than this early phase of his career. But that came nearly twenty years after George did this interview when the wounds had clearly healed.

That up-and-down attitude was there from early on,

not least because George was beginning to realize that he didn't want to be a cheesy pop star: he wanted to be cool. But that was never going to happen when he was taking shuttlecocks out of his shorts, and so at some stage a rethink would be needed. Wham! was very much of its time, but it couldn't go on forever, not that either bandmate wanted to stage a break just yet. "The time was right to strike home with Sixties escapism," George told *Rolling Stone*, in his interview published in November 1986, shortly after Wham! finally split for good. "Sixties presentation, Sixties attitude towards the songs. That's what made us big. Basically, we made everything look wonderful. Wham! was a Sixties pop group in the Eighties." But it came at a price. "I totally threw away my personal credibility for a year and a half in order to make sure my music got into so many people's homes," he continued. "It was a calculated risk, and I knew I would have to fight my way back from it. I did it out of choice."

It was some consolation that by this time the two of them were beginning to reap the financial rewards of pop superstardom. George bought a house in Kensington and a black Mercedes and the boys enjoyed a hedonistic lifestyle in the era of yuppiedom that both seemed to embody so well. But at heart, George knew it was not really him: "I created a man—in the image of a great friend—that the world could love if they chose to, someone who could realize my dreams and make me a star," he told the *Huffington Post* in 2009. "I called him George Michael, and for almost a decade, he worked his arse off for me, and did as he was told. He was very good at his job, perhaps a little too good."

As 1984 drew to a close, George and Andrew were back together as a team when it emerged they were planning to go for the Christmas Number 1 slot, always a coveted fixture in the pop music charts. Their main rivals of the time appeared to be Frankie Goes To Hollywood, who were at the height of their fame, producing edgier music than Wham!. The two outfits jousted with one another: "Careless Whisper" knocked Frankie's "Two Tribes" out of the top slot, while "Two Tribes" and "Relax," along with Stevie Wonder's "I Just Called To Say I Love You" and Band Aid's "Do They Know It's Christmas?," of which more below, kept "Careless Whisper" in fifth place in the UK bestselling singles of 1984.

Ironically, they were fronted by Frankie's lead vocalist Holly Johnson, about whose sexuality there was no speculation whatsoever: openly gay, he made no bones about it at all. Johnson was also not in the slightest bit concerned about shocking people: the video for the single "Relax," which was banned from the airwaves by the BBC (thus ensuring maximum publicity and a prolonged stint in the charts), looked like a mock-Roman orgy, with cages of transvestites and men in leather. It was a world away from clean-cut George and Andrew and of course there was no hint that George might even have been a little bit envious of rival singers who were allowed to flaunt their sexuality and make highly risqué videos. But he was also to have a considerably lengthier musical career than Johnson, who eventually became an artist.

And so it was to the race to the Christmas Number 1 slot and another song and video that came to define Wham! and indeed endures to this day. "Last Christmas/Everything She Wants" was a double A-side, but while both hits have endured it is "Last Christmas" that has become the classic, and perhaps, the best known song by George or Wham!, constantly reissued and covered by too many artists to list in full here. In fact, a website was launched a few years ago to track the cover versions and at the time of writing had found 135.

It was almost immediately accepted as one of the all-time Christmas classics and has never seen a drop in popularity from that day forward. The sleeve of the single featured George dressed as Santa Claus and Andrew as Rudolph the Red-nosed Reindeer (complete with shiny nose) and there was another memorable video to keep it in everyone's memory, because Wham! were nothing if not adept at translating their music into appealing visual form.

A group of extraordinarily attractive twenty-somethings, including of course George and Andrew, gather to celebrate Christmas in Alpine surroundings (actually Saas-Fee, Switzerland, which celebrated the thirtieth anniversary of filming by offering visits at 1980s prices and tours around locations shown in the film) and as the video progresses it becomes clear that Andrew's girlfriend (played by the model Kathy Hill) used to be George's girlfriend. There is more pouting melancholy from George along the same lines as in "Careless Whisper," but this time around he's the wronged one as opposed to the wrong-doer.

There is a flashback to the previous Christmas when George gave Kathy a brooch but in the end everyone appears to be paired up and happy. Trivia fans might want to take note that this is the last time George ever appeared clean-shaven on film; in the next video, "Everything She Wants," he had spouted designer stubble and was to keep a beard for the rest of his life. Pepsi and Shirlie were there, as was Spandau Ballet member Martin Kemp, who would go on to marry Shirlie in 1988, and, when they had children, name George as the godfather to their son Roman. The song, in fact, actually had almost nothing to do with Christmas: it was a ballad about a break-up that by chance happened at Christmas, but it has become such a seasonal staple that is often forgotten, and the video's scenes of snow and sipping chocolate by roaring fires did at least create a Noël-related atmosphere.

George had high hopes for the song. "As an artist, you want to reach as many people as possible," he told *Smash Hits* in 1984. "My aim is for our Christmas single—it's called 'Last Christmas'—to sell a million and a half. A great pop song has something about it that will appeal to millions of people. There are different ways of doing that. You can do it in a crass way like [the pineapple-happy single by the British pop band Black Lace] 'Agadoo,' or in an uplifting way like the way we do it in."

The single sold far more than he had even hoped:

over 2 million copies in the UK and another 750,000 in the US. It has become utterly standard Christmas fare and appears regularly in the charts every festive season around the world; in 2013, Spotify said it was the most streamed single on Christmas Day; in Germany it is the most successful Christmas song of all time, having spent 119 weeks in the charts and indeed having charted there every year since 1997; in the United States it is tenth on the list of all-time best-selling Christmas/holiday digital singles in US SoundScan history. And of course it was given an extra poignancy in 2016, when George himself died on Christmas Day.

Would it get to Number 1? More on that shortly. In the meantime, it is worth restating the single was actually a double A-side, with "Everything She Wants" being another take on male/female relationships, this time a disillusioned one as George takes on the role of a man who cannot do enough for his materialistic partner because she is simply never satisfied. As an added twist, he then discovers she is pregnant—"[but] if his best is not enough for one, how can it be enough for two?" George actually cited this as his favorite Wham! song and, unlike some of his other early hits, continued to play it when he gave solo concerts. Chris Porter also gave an insight into how it came about: "Quite often he'll start a song with a verse or a chorus and nothing else. And then he'll build that up day by day," he told *Rolling Stone* in 1986. "He elaborated on it ['Everything She Wants'] over about four days until it became a complete song." It also became the title of a volume of Charles Moore's biography of Margaret Thatcher, so much did it seem to exemplify the 1980s.

"Last Christamas" never did reach the Number 1 spot. The song that did triumph was "Do They Know It's Christmas?" by Bob Geldof and Midge Ure, sung by a hastily formed supergroup called Band Aid and released in order to raise aid for the Ethiopian famine. Some of the biggest names of the era sang on that record, including its two composers, as well as Bono, Sting, Paul Young, Phil Collins, Martin Kemp and various other members of Spandau Ballet, Simon Le Bon and his Duran Duran bandmates, Bananarama, Paul Weller and George Michael himself, which means that he did get his Christmas Number 1, albeit not in the form he was expecting. Wham! gave the proceeds of "Last Christmas/Everything She Wants" to charity, to fight the Ethiopian famine, too.

## 5

# CONQUERING CHINA

By the beginning of 1985, Wham! had made its presence felt throughout the world—with one enormous exception. China was still perceived to be hostile to Western culture, especially pop music, but winds of change were blowing and it was becoming apparent that the government wanted to encourage foreign investment. How better to show that times were changing than to allow a Western pop group to perform? And so the race began to be the first-ever Western pop group to play in China, an event that would spread many, many more ripples than a normal pop concert because it would signify not just another country and another set of fans for the group involved, but an actual desire by the Chinese government to open itself up to influences from the West.

It had never been done before and manager Simon

Napier-Bell was determined that it would be Wham! who led the way, but he was up against some very stiff competition, including the Rolling Stones. Napier-Bell opened negotiations with Chinese officials, and when he heard that the group Queen was also hoping to be a pioneer, he reacted by taking a photograph of Queen front man Freddie Mercury in all his decadent glory and compared that to the wholesome-looking George Michael and Andrew Ridgeley. It was a move that won the day.

The boys were to play two dates: one at the Workers' Gymnasium in Beijing, followed by the southern city of Guangzhou. When the first of these concerts, part of their world tour, took place in April 1985 no one knew what to expect. There had never been a pop concert in China before; indeed, the Chinese people had been actively discouraged from listening to pop. It wasn't so much a culture clash as a cultural upheaval. These days "Careless Whisper" is an absolute standard all across China, but it had yet to be heard back then. And unlikely as it sounded, the duo from the suburbs of London, now two of the most famous men in the world, were to be Britain's cultural ambassadors, roles they took on with customary panache.

If truth be told, although it was an important and ground-breaking cultural event, the initial concert, in front of 15,000 people, did not actually go that well. Kan Lijun, who has since become a well-known television presenter, introduced the act. "No one had ever seen anything like that before," she told the BBC in April 2015. "The singers were all moving a lot and it was very loud. We were used to people who stood still when they performed. All the young people were amazed and everybody was tapping their feet. Of course the police weren't happy and they were scared there would be riots. One time, people were excited after a sports event and they flipped a car. Back then if we wanted to listen to pop music with lyrics like that, we had to do that in secret. If you were caught, you would be taken to the police station and they would keep you there all night. It was a time of many taboos."

George and Andrew tried their hardest, but a lot of the time the audience had no idea how to respond. Simon Napier-Bell recalled that George tried to get the audience to clap along to "Club Tropicana." "But they hadn't a clue—they thought he wanted applause and politely gave it." Some caught on a little faster and did "get the hang of clapping on the beat, even learnt to scream when George or Andrew waved their bums."

But it was something of an ordeal: not understanding the different cultural mores, Napier-Bell sent a breakdancer into the crowd, which actually caused some considerable problems. "The powers that be were just horrified at this," he told the BBC in 2005. "In the interval, they announced on the loudspeaker that nobody could stand up, everyone had to sit down through the whole show—which was 100 per cent my fault. I really killed the atmosphere." Matters were made worse by people sitting on the ground level fearing that camera crews were actually secret police: "There were 7,500 people downstairs intimidated by the lights and the police standing around the outside, and upstairs you had 7,500 people getting more and more wild and crazy," said Simon. "So it was a very strange atmosphere." But it served its purpose. "In the end everybody got what they wanted from it," he told the *Taipei Times* in April 2005. "Wham! became the biggest, most famous band in the world and the Chinese got a concert that proved they meant what they said about opening up."

But some cultural mores didn't change immediately: many people received tickets because of their connection to the Chinese government. "I went to see it because my classmate's father worked for the Ministry of Culture and I was given a free ticket," Lin Wenjun from Guangzhou told the BBC in April 2015. "Not many people knew about them at the time but I listened to their music on Hong Kong radio, which wasn't blocked back then. It seemed that most of the audience received free tickets because they seemed old. They didn't dress like music lovers. Before that day, I had only seen a ballet performance. So the concert was a shocking experience because of all the lights and the stereo sound. I wanted to sing along with the lyrics but I didn't dare because no-one else in the audience was singing."

But others were there in the more conventional way: they saw ads for the tickets and bought them. If they were allowed to by their parents, that is. One thing that China did have in common with the West was an older generation concerned about the pernicious influence of pop stars: George and Andrew might have been pretty clean-living examples of the genre (back then at least) but the older generation could still be suspicious of the younger one.

"One day, I saw the concert announcement posted on a wall," Li Shizhong from Beijing, a teenager when the event took place, told the BBC. "The band members had long curly hair. They dressed differently. I thought their music would sound different and new because they looked so different from anything else I had seen before. But I couldn't go to see them because I couldn't ask my parents for five yuan ($0.80) to pay for the ticket. My parents wouldn't support anything like that. We didn't have a nightlife. I was a 15-year-old boy but I had to stay at home after 8:30 p.m. The rigid social atmosphere back then was the real reason I couldn't go to the concert. At that time, if you played a guitar on the street, you would be considered a hooligan. I only had blue, green and grey Cultural Revolution style clothes. If someone dressed in a different color, everyone would notice. Now we think that's fashionable, but back then, something like that signalled trouble."

Such was the importance attached to the concerts that even the British Embassy got in on the act. That this was utterly unprecedented meant that a senior civil servant was sent along to write notes on what happened and it makes for entertaining reading. "The Workers' Gymnasium was almost filled and the concert, generally speaking, seems to have been a success," the first secretary to the British Embassy wrote in a report about the event.

"In deference to their Chinese audience, Wham! kept the volume of the music rather lower than normal, but there was overall a certain lack of mutual understanding. Neither the Chinese nor Wham! knew quite how to behave faced with something completely beyond their experience. There was some lively dancing but this was almost entirely confined to younger Western members of the audience. Some Chinese did make the effort, but they were discouraged in this by the police. They were unable to deal satisfactorily with the younger Westerners but they did on the whole manage to keep the Chinese in their place." Fortunately, he concluded, it all went well. "There is no reason to suppose that the Chinese have been discouraged by their experience... Financially they must have done very well," he wrote. "There was certainly considerable interest by the younger Chinese in the visit. There was a lively black market in tickets for the concert, although this was no doubt encouraged by Wham!'s generosity in giving a free copy of their latest tape away with each ticket."

That tape was itself a curiosity. It featured Wham! songs on one side and cover versions sung in Chinese by Cheng Fangyuan on the other. The translations were sometimes interesting: the Chinese version of "Wake Me Up Before You Go-Go," for example, contained the following lines:

"Wake me up before you go go/Compete with the sky to go high, high/Wake me up before you go go/Men fight to be first to reach the peak/Wake me up before you go go/Women are on the same journey and will not fall behind."

There was a second, rather more successful concert in Guangzhou—at least everyone had some small idea of what to expect now—while George and Andrew, all bouffant-haired and fizzing with energy, posed for portraits beside the Great Wall of China and other famous attractions. It was a change for them: rather than being mobbed as they were in the West, this time the Chinese kept a respectful distance. But something very profound had changed for good and one of the people responsible was Simon Napier-Bell, who had driven the whole project ahead.

"In the early to mid-1980s, China was still very much recovering its composure after the years of isolation and cultural madness," Andrew Bull, a music impresario based in Shanghai, told TIME in December 2016. "Really early adopters had started going to Beijing for New Year's Eve, and there were a few hotels opening up, but it was still the era of the bicycles and the green outfits and everything. Simon, the guy who did the Wham! thing, was way ahead, light years ahead. The guy's a legend on a whole other level. He had the vision and the chutzpah to glue the unlikely thing together and he must have found the right Chinese people at the right time to make that happen. If you look at the video now it's amazing—you know, George and Andrew running around Beijing in a Red Flag limo."

The video referred to was a film, *Wham! In China: Foreign Skies* (1986), directed by Lindsay Anderson—or at least it was until he left after a series of rows with George—and produced by Martin Lewis. The common consensus was that it didn't really work. "It's a peculiar film, and not an especially good one," wrote Glenn Dunks of *Film Experience*. "Half Chinese travelogue for the Western audiences; half concert film focusing, rightly, on the energetic and handsome George Michael sashaying around on stage like nobody had ever seen before." At the same time, the single "Freedom" was released in the United States, featuring a video of the boys in China, which had received global coverage—with most of the attention, as was standard by this time, centering on George.

Indeed, so much attention was paid to George that there had begun to be some alarm that he did not appear to have a significant other. Why, it was asked, should a handsome young man with the world at his feet be forced to be alone? And so there was great excitement when he was spotted with the beautiful American actress Brooke Shields. The two met in 1985 and went on a few dates, starting at the rooftop of a Chicago hotel. Brooke gave a rather tongue-in-cheek account of their "relationship" in her 2014 autobiography, *There Was A Little Girl: The Real Story Of My Mother And Me*: "Nobody had ever been willing to move so slowly. It must be love," she wrote, confiding she was at that point still a virgin and didn't want to be rushed into anything. George was "a remarkable, respectful and patient gentleman who was obviously aware of my hesitance regarding sex... he left without even trying to kiss me. I was so touched by what a real gentleman he was." When the "relationship" broke up shortly afterwards, it was blamed on media intrusion.

Officially, at least, it was back to business as usual, but behind the scenes it was increasingly apparent that Wham! had run its natural course. George so dominated everything they did that a solo future was assured and whatever he might have thought of "Careless Whisper," if it had been seen as a test run as to how well he could do on his own, it was a test passed with flying colors. Increasingly, it became a matter of not if but when. Meanwhile, Andrew grew more interested in motor racing as George began working on more solo projects.

One of these, interestingly, was with David Cassidy, the star of *The Partridge Family* TV series (1970–74), who in later years would also suffer from problems with alcohol and a heavy fall from grace. And when the two men actually did work together, it was a decade after Cassidy's own days as a major teen heartthrob were over, although he was still seeing some professional success. But it was a curious choice for George, not least because he was coming to resent his own status as a teen heartthrob and wanted to be taken more seriously, which begged the question of why he was working with the man whose greatest hit to this day remains "I Think I Love You." Of course it is entirely possible that he also wanted Cassidy's advice on how to break out of the niche he had carved for himself and become a serious artist.

The number in question was "The Last Kiss" on David's 1985 album *Romance*. "I'm still proud of the record," Cassidy told Culturebrats.com. "In fact, a little known fact, it was George Michael who I began working with and co-producing some stuff with and actually sang background on it, and he did a great job. He's a terrific artist. At the time, he was just leaving Wham! It was right before his first solo album got gigantic and I enjoyed working with him." The sentiment was more than reciprocated: disclosing that the two had met because they shared a music publisher, Dick Leahy, George actually interviewed Cassidy in June 1985 for the *Ritz* newspaper, a trendy magazine that ran for fifteen years from 1976. Cassidy was a "major career influence" said George, although he might of course have been thinking of the singer-songwriter's attempts to reinvent himself.

Although the piece purports to be George interviewing David, it certainly gives a pretty good indication of the former's state of mind. "Don't you find that if your image was one thing," George asked rather pointedly, "if you have been created or are part of something which creates an image, that when you try to do anything which is even vaguely upsetting to that image, even though it's really you, people see it as false, which is very frustrating, obviously?"

Or (talking about Cassidy's re-emergence into the music scene): "I think, having seen some reviews of the stuff, there are a lot of sympathetic ears and there are a lot of people who would slag you off for no reason. There are also people that would give it an open ear or even a biased beneficial opinion because they have memories of you from their youth and everything, like through rose-colored glasses."

Or: "Was there a point when you said to yourself, 'I really miss it?' That is the fascination for me. Every time I think it's getting too much for me, and I'm not enjoying being part of everyone's lives, I do have to say to myself what would my real reaction be if in two years from now I hadn't been in a paper for a year."

Apparently, it took Cassidy several years before he missed being in the newspapers but that wasn't really the point. The interview is far more revealing about what was on George's mind than that of his subject. Other topics included fear of burnout, something else that appeared to be of concern. Somewhat ominously, given what was to happen to both of them, George gleefully related that after the interview the pair got riotously drunk.

Meanwhile, George's extracurricular activities continued. He did some work with Elton John; the beginning of a complicated relationship which was to have its own ups and downs. One track was 'Nikita', from Elton's 1985 *Ice*

*On Fire* album. It describes a crush on an East German bodyguard (played in the accompanying video by a woman), who Elton can never meet as he isn't allowed into the country. George and Nik Kershaw provide backing vocals.

George contributed similarly on Elton's song "Wrap Her Up" from the same album, saying memorably at the time to *Smash Hits* that "it sounded like I had my willy in a garrotte" because of the falsetto he sang in. Goodness knows what kind of denial or indeed in-joke the crew were in on for a whole roll call of famous women are cited and drooled over at the end: Marlene Dietrich, Rita Hayworth, Marilyn Monroe, Katharine Hepburn, Dusty Springfield, Billie Jean King, Vanessa Williams, Nancy Reagan, Julie Andrews, Annie Lennox, Shirley Temple, Tallulah Bankhead, Princess Caroline of Monaco, Little Eva, Mata Hari, Joan Collins, Brigitte Bardot, Doris Day, Samantha Fox and Priscilla Presley. Kiki Dee, with whom Elton duetted at an earlier stage ("Don't Go Breaking My Heart," 1976), was also a backing singer; she appears at the end of the video to have Elton smash a cream pie in her face. It was no one's finest hour.

Both George and Andrew appeared in the Wembley Stadium Live Aid concert in July 1985, again in aid of famine-struck Ethiopia. Tellingly, they did not perform together per se. Rather, George and Elton performed "Don't Let The Sun Go Down On Me," while Andrew and Kiki Dee were two of the backing singers. Again and again it was obvious that something was going to change. By then, Andrew's motor racing had become more serious —he was spending a lot of time in Monaco and was also thinking of launching an acting career. There was even talk of fatherhood. He, too, was ready for a change.

With George now openly seeking satisfaction in other work, the split became increasingly certain and despite the fact that there were to be inevitable tensions between George and Andrew, it was painful. After all, they had been friends since they were twelve and they had been able to rely on each other amid all the madness. Slowly, inexorably, the end was near, and this became all the more apparent when George issued another solo single, "A Different Corner," which appeared on an album titled *Music From The Edge of Heaven*—which is only available in Japan and North America—as well as the boys' compilation album, *The Final*, with which they bade their fans goodbye. George, who was still nominally a member of Wham! when the single was released, found himself in the unusual position both of being in a group and also becoming the first ever solo artist whose two first releases charted at No. 1 in the UK charts. It was also the second No. 1 (after Stevie Wonder's "I Just Called To Say I Love You") to be written, sung, played, arranged and produced by the same artist and if George was using it to test the waters to see how he would fare solo, there was no cause for concern. Apart from the single charting all over the world, the BBC DJ Simon Bates liked it so much that, after playing it for the first time, he immediately went back and played it again from the start. George was still the golden boy; he certainly hadn't lost his magic touch.

The inevitable could no longer be postponed. In the spring of 1986, George and Andrew made the announcement that those behind the scenes already knew was coming: Wham! were to split up. They would release one last single together, "The Edge of Heaven" (Elton played piano on the record), there would be a farewell album, *The Final*, followed by one last concert at London's Wembley Stadium, and then that would be that. The dream conjured up by a couple of schoolboys would be over and they would go it alone.

"The Edge of Heaven" purported to be about an emotionally abusive heterosexual relationship and George said that it was deliberately much edgier than previous Wham! songs as that was the direction in which he wanted to go. But the opening lines signalled a much deeper turmoil within the songwriter than anyone had been aware of previously: "I would lock you up / But I could not bear to hear you / Screaming to be set free." Was he talking about Andrew? Or himself? Dressed in white, sitting in a white room and singing wistfully, it was impossible to fathom what was really on George's mind.

George was beginning to loathe the persona he'd created for himself, as was evident in his conversation with David Cassidy, and while inner torment about his sexuality was growing worse, he was nowhere near resolving the issue —he even had a girlfriend after Wham! split up. Nor did his record company seem that keen on promoting the new tortured George: they released the song as part of a double set, with the flip side featuring an updated version of "Wham Rap! (Enjoy What You Do)." The second disc featured "Battlestations" and "Where Did Your Heart Go?," a cover of a song by the American group Was (Not Was).

It was another Number 1 in the UK and elsewhere, while the aptly named album *The Final* got to No. 2. The bandmates were determined their personal relationship should not suffer any more than it was likely bound to do, given that George was continuing with his musical career and Andrew was not: "I think it should be the most amicable split in pop history," George told *Smash Hits* in July 1986. Later, he was to express some considerable anger at what he felt was unfair treatment of Andrew: some sections of the media had been down on him, he snarled. The bond between them was still there.

But speculation of another kind was beginning to appear in the press, too. Until then the story had always been put about that George Michael was a rampant womanizer. For the first time, though, some doubts were cast. The *Sun* had tracked down a musician called Colin Graham, who claimed he'd only seen George with a girl once and that the next day George had said, "There was nothing between her ears to turn me on—a decent mind is better than a decent body any day." According to Graham, George was a "real mummy's boy" and he added a story about a birthday surprise strip-o-gram: "She stood there, in stockings and suspenders, and sang this real naff birthday song we'd composed for him. George was absolutely speechless. He went bright red and began stuttering uncontrollably. Then he literally turned tail and ran off the stage and hid until she'd gone. It was unbelievable. He was a millionaire heartthrob and he was behaving like a blushing schoolboy..." George certainly wouldn't have been the first person to be discomfited by a stripper and if anything the story does him credit. But it was a clear hint that all was not as it seemed.

As the countdown to the split began, there was a surprise performance at Brixton Academy, Wham!'s last *Top Of The Pops* shindig and then, on June 28, 1986, the boys took to the stage for their final concert, a sold-out affair for 72,000 fans. It took place on a boiling-hot day and went on for eight hours, with supporting acts and a sometimes hysterical crowd.

All the hits were played and they did an encore of "I'm Your Man" accompanied by Duran Duran's Simon Le Bon. At the end of it all a clearly emotional George and Andrew embraced one another. "Thanks, George, I'm going to cry now," said Andrew.

After five years of madness, Wham! was at an end.

# CONQUERING CHINA

# 6

# GOING SOLO

And so, it had finally happened. One of the most successful pop acts of the 1980s had split up, the only British act of the decade to secure three Number 1s in both the UK and the US, with its component members setting off in dramatically different directions. George was determined to make it even bigger while Andrew continued his motor racing, dabbled in acting and had a short-lived solo singing career, mainly because of contractual obligations stemming from his Wham! days. He was occasionally to appear on stage with George in the coming years but in 1990, after stints in Monaco and Los Angeles, he returned to the UK and settled in Cornwall with his long-term partner Keren Woodward of Bananarama. Ridgeley gives every indication of contentment, with a fortune based on Wham! royalties of an estimated £10 million to £25 million, depending on whom you believe. George would speak wistfully of Andrew's contented domestic set-up in the years that lay ahead. A very different fate lay in store for George, however.

The two men never fell out—far from it—although in the immediate aftermath of the split, George was brutally realistic about the way it had panned out between them. As far as he was concerned, Andrew was the person who had got Wham! up and running, but it was he who had become the creative force. "He knew he was coasting," he told *Rolling Stone* in November 1986. "We both knew it. But we never lied to anybody about it. What people wouldn't accept was that Wham! was a vehicle, a successful image—two kids who strike it lucky. We never said we were a songwriting duo. Okay, Andrew doesn't sing. But we're accepting that. It's just that nobody else would. We kept trying to say, 'We're good friends, we started playing together, people like us together.' Wham! was working brilliantly. It was working for both of us. It was no con."

It was working so brilliantly that George actually went through a difficult period after Wham! split up: if anything, for a brief time it seemed as if Andrew was the one who had the workable plan. Tellingly, it was to him that George turned in his distress in the wake of the break-up and it was Andrew who got him going again.

"The actual Wham! split was definitely provoked by my emotional distress around that period," George told *Rolling Stone* in 1988. "It's hard to tell whether or not it would have happened at that time had it not been for that relationship failing [George had spoken earlier in the interview of an elusive woman who had spurned his advances]. Maybe if I'd felt more secure, I would have felt no need to shake things up. But at the time I just wanted to make a clear start. Basically, I didn't want to be a star anymore, because I was feeling so sorry for myself."

"I think George had come close to doing almost everything he wanted to do," Andrew added in the same interview, "but it really hadn't worked out quite as planned. And then there was that emotional involvement that turned sour. He had a fairly rough ride for a while, I think. He leans to introspection, and he's very analytical, and he screws himself up on that a lot. I don't think his attitude to life is very carefree."

George spent the best part of a year drinking too much in locations all over the globe before a night out with Andrew that the latter described as "his exorcism." "[Andrew] just got the whole lot, every awful feeling that I was having," George recalled to *Rolling Stone*. "And then the next day it was just gone. Vanished, to the degree that I couldn't believe it. I kept expecting it to creep back on me, but it never did."

"I won't say it could have been anyone," said Andrew (actually, it almost certainly couldn't have been), "but George just needed a shoulder to cry on, in its simplest sense. That night in L.A. it came to a head, he got it out, and I think he grew up a bit and realized that you have to get on with things."

Another change that happened back then was that George's public persona went from carefree to tortured, although it took a while for people to notice. "I can't pretend I'm a young man with no problems any more," he told the press. Wham! was "built on a careless, upbeat image of fair-haired, suntanned boys singing about love without pain… The test is now to come across much more as a real person."

There were other challenges, too. Although no one realized it at the time, George had other issues on his mind. The drip, drip of insinuation had begun that, despite his ladies' man image, there didn't actually appear to be many ladies on the scene. Did George, perhaps, have something to hide?

George tackled it head-on, in a kind of double bluff. Hint at the truth and hope that that will head off the inquiries. "People do keep telling me there's a story, but I can't think what it would be," he told *NME* in 1986. "The *News Of The World*'s angle would have to be, if it's big enough that they're waiting, some kind of gay story. Either that or a pregnant girl. It's unnerving to think that they're only waiting because they think the public likes me enough at the moment. Hopefully they've got a long wait, and even then I'll sue the arse off them, ha ha!"

But of course it must have been weighing horribly on his mind, not least because Culture Club star Boy George, who once famously (and inaccurately) declared that he preferred "a nice cup of tea" to sex had recently been outed as being addicted to heroin and there were rumors his personal life was not as straightforward as it seemed. Boy George had never denied being gay but he had not at this stage confirmed it either—like his near namesake it was going to take courage to come out of the closet and it would be a while before he felt able to do so. The 1980s, for all its hedonism, was not an era in which it was easy to acknowledge one's homosexuality.

Indeed, in that same interview George was asked if negative coverage could harm a career and there was one person very much on his mind: "It can accelerate it terribly. With Boy George they accelerated it," he said. "If you're being cheeky with the public and playing with their affections, and the press jumps on you at the same time, you're beyond the point of no return. George is going to have to work fucking hard to get people back, you know. If a person respects the fact that the public has put them where they are, and if they don't realize the public have always got that in mind—you owe something to the public—you start mucking around with the reasons for your success. That's not to say you need to pander to the public. All you need to do is give them quality and don't offend them. If you feel bad about the way the public is treating you, just shut up about it – they don't care about the way you feel. You have to be careful with the public the way you have to be careful with someone who's had a few drinks, d'you know what I mean? You be nice to them and they'll be wonderful, you can have a good laugh with them. But if you annoy them then you're going to get the worst side!"

He was as near as telling anyone who cared to listen that he had a few issues of his own, but if truth be told the public didn't want to hear. They had loved seeing George and Andrew as two young men out on the town partying and if the reality was a little different, well, they didn't want to have to deal with it. Instead, there was a great deal of curiosity as to what George was going to do next. He had been adamant that he wanted a solo career, now was the chance to prove that he could do it. And he did, but curiously enough, he kicked off with a duet. It was almost as if he was testing the waters to see how he would do: he no longer had Andrew Ridgeley in the background to provide emotional stability and support, and it should be remembered that even when he did release his earlier solo numbers, Andrew was still very much around, and so he turned elsewhere. And that elsewhere was to Aretha Franklin, the most renowned soul singer of her generation.

George had long wanted to perform with her. Additionally, this proved that his voice was good enough to hold its own when up against one of the greats. And so "I Knew You Were Waiting (For Me)" went straight to Number 1 in both the UK and the US charts. It became George's third consecutive solo hit, Aretha's only UK No. 1 and, to date, the last of her seventeen Top 10 hits in the States. The accompanying video was charming enough: it had George and two bodyguards entering a room in which there was a video playing of Aretha getting ready to meet George. The two gradually wend their way towards one another, on screen and off, ending with a big wink from Aretha. It was also marked by a few other oddities: it was the first single George had sung as a solo artist that he had not actually written himself (more testing the waters, perhaps) and its co-writer, Simon Climie, later went on to become a performer himself, as part of pop duo Climie Fisher. The number was also to win George and Aretha a Grammy Award in 1988 for Best R&B Performance – Duo or Group with Vocal. It was a good start.

But more was needed. George wanted to be a serious solo artist, with the emphasis on "serious." And so he set to work on the album and single that was to blow his squeaky-clean image out of the water: the album *Faith* and its provocative, controversial first single "I Want Your Sex." "I Want Your Sex," came out in June 1987. These days the lyrics do not seem worthy of causing the uproar they did at the time ("Sex is natural / Sex is good / Not everybody does it / But everybody should") but it was the accompanying video, directed by Andy Morahan, that really raised eyebrows. In the Wham! videos there was plenty of cavorting with girls, but in this case it was of a different order: there was a lot of writhing around in black satin sheets, use of blindfolds and shots of a very comely woman in black lingerie.

Two women were actually involved in the making of the video, while George is seen writing "explore" and "monogamy" on the legs of one of them, somewhat ironic given his later attitude towards that particular way of life. It was the first-ever pop song with the word "sex" in the title (in 1982 Marvin Gaye's "Sexual Healing" came close but it wasn't quite there) and there was some nervousness about the release.

The song and video caused an absolute uproar. Some radio stations banned it and the BBC refused to play it until after 9 p.m. This was the era of AIDS, a life-threatening syndrome that was still not fully understood, and it seemed to many that it was crassly irresponsible to promote such hedonism at a time when people were, literally, dying from it. Indeed, there was such a row over the music channel MTV showing the video that they were forced to publish a disclaimer from George: "The media has divided love and sex incredibly. The emphasis of the AIDS campaign has been on safe sex, but the campaign has missed relationships. It's missed emotion. It's missed monogamy. 'I Want Your Sex' is about attaching lust to love, not just to strangers."

Whatever the media was doing, George's profile was soaring ever higher because of all the publicity and fuel added to the fire when it emerged that a US radio station was amending the track themselves so it actually became "I Want Your Love." They were sending copies to George's record company, Columbia. "In no way, shape or form would George endorse any edit like that—he's absolutely opposed to it," Rob Kahane, one of Michael's managers, told the *Los Angeles Times* in June 1987. "We don't want the song altered at all. Anyone that does is (messing) with George's music." Some DJs could not bring themselves to say the title: the America Top 40 host Casey Kasem would only call it "the new single by George Michael."

But Kahane, as much as anyone, was well aware what good publicity this was for someone who wanted to change their image and it wasn't exactly harming record sales, either. "All the odds were against something like this [the image change] happening," he told the *LA Times*. "If they had to lay money down a year and a half ago on him being successful, most people would have laid it against him."

Freddy DeMann, Madonna and Lionel Richie's manager, agreed: "It's just a matter of growth," said DeMann in an *LA Times* article dating from 1988. "Some people were dismissing Madonna after the first album and into the second album, but she's gotten more respect over the years. I think George is doing the same thing. Every artist has to grow and I think both of them have the innate talent to do it. There are others who don't and they fall by the wayside."

"That [record] was a turning point in the way people perceive George Michael as an artist," Kahane added. "It was the first time since I've been involved in George's career that people were asking serious questions about his music."

Oddly enough, although it was to prove one of George's biggest hits, he appeared to be taking the same attitude to it as he did towards "Careless Whisper." There was a Faith tour, of course, but after the tour he dropped the song from his repertoire. It is impossible to say why, but perhaps it had something to do with the fact that the woman with whom he was pictured writhing around on the video was the Asian model Kathy Jeung, who for a short time was presented as George's girlfriend. George, after he had come out, was adamant that she really was his girlfriend and that she knew he was bisexual; Kathy certainly spoke warmly about him after his death, writing in one post: "with no exaggeration, he was the most generous, hilarious, brilliant, talented, #truefriend."

Those in the know, of course, were well aware of the reality of the situation, but there was a continuing reluctance to risk such a major star coming out as gay. George's sisters, Melanie and Yioda, already knew, but were concerned about the impact George going public would have on their father. Nor did record-industry figures wish to rock the boat. And given that this was the AIDS era, there were concerns about how that would play with the public as well.

But this secrecy and the level of double-think it required was almost bound to make everything worse. In the early Wham! days there had been the stories of sex with numerous groupies; now his adult breakthrough had come on the back of a video in which he was seen cavorting with a woman with whom, the world was told, he was having a passionate relationship. This was not the real George. All this was to exact a terrible toll, but given how young he was—still in his mid-twenties—neither he nor anyone else realized that living a lie to the extent that he was doing was going to exact a terrible price in the longer term. Not only did he know what the reality was and was forced to pretend that it was something different, but there was the constant fear of exposure. It was beginning to happen quite a lot now in interviews that he was asked whether the rumors were true, but still he couldn't bring himself to confirm his sexuality. Naturally, this was a recipe for future mental-health issues and so it proved.

George became well aware of this, too. "My depression at the end of Wham! was because I was beginning to realize I was gay, not bi," he told the *Huffington Post* much later on, in February 2009. "I felt cornered by my own ambition. I didn't have the self-control to restrain my ego, but I knew it was leading me further and further towards an explosive end. I was becoming absolutely massively popular as a heterosexual male. It hadn't occurred to me, when I went solo, that I would get a whole new generation of 13-year-old girls [as fans] from *Faith*, but it happened. And in here..."—he touched his chest—"in here, I was gay."

Not to the wider public, though, who now saw him as a cute young boy turned raunchy sex symbol. "I Want Your Sex" might have been his way of creating a more adult image, but it also added to the burden of secrecy: how on earth could he come out after that? And so he didn't.

Instead, he brought out the next single from the album, the title track "Faith." This hinted at raunch as well ("Well I guess it would be nice / If I could touch your body") but there was a far more innocent feel to it, much more reminiscent of traditional rock 'n' roll. It, too, was a huge hit, not only getting to Number 1 in the States, but also becoming the Number 1 record for the whole of 1988. The song reached Number 2 in the UK and there was another attention-catching video—again affirming the image of George as a straight sex symbol, dressed in shades, Levis and cowboy boots, trademark stubble in place and playing his guitar beside a classic Wurlitzer jukebox. The image was designed to ooze masculinity and it did.

The hit singles kept on coming: "Hard Day," "Father Figure" (the video had George as a cab driver with a supermodel, Tania Coleridge, in his car; the lyrics also hinted at quite a different kind of relationship—"I will be your father figure / I will be your preacher teacher") "One More Try," "Monkey," "Kissing A Fool." There was the odd upset: "Father Figure" only got to No. 11 in the UK, the first time George had failed to get into the Top 10 in his homeland, but his popularity continued to grow in leaps and bounds. He had done what he set out to do: he was now a fully acclaimed serious musician, the equal of anyone on the pop scene, and showing no signs at all of slowing down.

The reviewers agreed this had been a real breakthrough. AllMusic critic Steve Huey said *Faith* was a "superbly crafted mainstream pop/rock masterpiece... one of the finest pop albums of the '80s." *Rolling Stone*'s Mark Coleman said "[It] displays Michael's intuitive understanding of pop music and his increasingly intelligent use of his power to communicate to an ever-growing audience." "The first solo album by George Michael should go a long way toward dispelling the public perception of the 24-year-old alumnus of Wham! as just another pretty-boy pop star from England," wrote the *Chicago Tribune*.

George was in fact now starting to be seen as not just another good singer-songwriter but one of the all-time greats: his was a special talent, it was now obvious, and if he continued at this rate then he would be on course for one of the all-time great pop careers. "I think it says something for the power of the music," he told *Rolling Stone* in a major interview after the success of *Faith*, "that I've managed to change the perception of what I do to the degree that I have in this short a time. Because it's something that a lot of people thought wasn't possible."

And his former bandmate was delighted by this turn of events, too. "George is very, very single-minded in his approach," Andrew Ridgeley, then living in Monaco, told *Rolling Stone*. "And I think a lot of the things that he has said and done have been misconstrued as arrogant rather than the single-mindedness they really are. People get very put out when someone is as forceful in their views and in their methods as George is."

And so George set off on his first major solo tour,

a massive undertaking of 137 shows worldwide that quickly sold out. It was choreographed by Paula Abdul and consolidated George's status as a bona fide superstar, able to command the stage as a solo performer while also delighting fans with some songs from the old days, including "Everything She Wants." In Los Angeles, he was joined on stage by Aretha Franklin for a duet of "I Knew You Were Waiting (For Me)" and, in Birmingham, an episode that obviously moved him, a mystery guest came onstage. The date was June 25, 1988, George's twenty-fifth birthday, and he was playing the third of three dates at the NEC. Quite suddenly, and to George's obvious surprise, Andrew Ridgeley appeared in the wings, surrounded by members of George's family, and proceeded to push a huge trolley onstage, topped with a birthday cake. They led the 13,000-strong audience in singing "Happy Birthday" to George, after which Andrew joined him in a rendition of "I'm Your Man." It was a touching moment.

Reviewers loved it. "It wasn't a show, it was an attempted seduction," wrote the *Los Angeles Times*. "Michael combines the instincts of a soul singer with the moves of a male go-go dancer. While wailing away on such sizzling dance tunes as 'Monkey,' 'Faith' and 'I'm Your Man,' he was bumping, grinding and strutting like one of those hunks on the runway at Chippendales." The *Miami Herald* felt that, "George Michael turned the Orange Bowl into a steaming, bubbling caldron of horniness Saturday night."

The Faith tour was a stupendous undertaking. It lasted the best part of a year and a half, kicking off in February 1988 and finally coming to an end in July 1989. George toured Europe, North America, Australia, Asia and New Zealand. Meanwhile the album stayed at the top of the charts and he made that all-important transition into serious artist—while paying a heavy price.

In retrospect it is quite clear that this was George Michael at the absolute peak of his powers and although much more success awaited him, he would never quite scale these dizzy heights again. For a start, the sheer amount of stamina required was astonishing and secondly, he had to share this burden on his own. Until then he'd always had Andrew Ridgeley with him for moral support. It was a lot to bear on his own and it was when this tour ended that George began the gradual retreat from the public eye which would continue for the rest of his life.

More than that, however, the dichotomy between his public image and private reality was stretching to a breaking point. In its 1988 review of a Madison Square Garden concert, the *New York Times* wrote, "Behind his stubble, his black leather jacket, his dangling-crucifix earring and his pirate-style head scarf, George Michael—or the character he plays in his songs—is the kind of guy most teenage girls could bring home to meet the folks. In a way, many of them have; his album *Faith* has sold nearly five million copies, and screams and shrieks greeted almost every move when he performed Sunday at Madison Square Garden, where he opened a sold-out three-night stand. As he has been since he led the British pop group Wham!, Mr. Michael is still a teen idol, although he doesn't seem thrilled at the idea; early in the concert, he asked the audience to be quiet during ballads."

Behind the scenes, of course, something very different was playing out. George wouldn't, or couldn't, come out to his fans just yet, but in some circles people were beginning to call him "Coy George" in reference to Boy George, who had also had a hard time before he too came out. It would be years before George was able to tell the public that he was gay, and by the time he did so, the strain of living a lie for so long had finally got to him. Drama, much, much more drama, lay ahead.

# GOING SOLO

7

# SOMETIMES THE CLOTHES DO NOT MAKE THE MAN

With a huge amount of success comes a huge amount of scrutiny and by the start of the 1990s, George Michael had been in the eye of the storm for the best part of a decade. The intensity of the interest in him had actually grown over the years, not declined, partly out of admiration for the way he had turned himself from a teeny-bopper idol into a mature performer, but also because of all those rumors that refused to go away about his private life. The Faith tour had intensified that still further and by the end of it George was mentally and physicall exhausted. He had no desire to do that again in a hurry and was about to make as much plain. But the conversation he had had with David Cassidy back in 1985 was an indication of what was really worrying him: on the one hand he wanted all the attention to go away while, on the other, would he really be happy if people were not interested in what he was doing any more?

Although the demons that would torment George had their roots in his childhood, they came about more because of the struggle over his sexuality than the tussles with his father and now, having established himself as one of the most popular and successful entertainers in the world, his relationship with his father had markedly improved. It is common for teenage boys to take on their fathers. Indeed, for many it is a rite of passage. Now that George was nearing thirty he had proven to his father that'd he'd made the right decision as a teenager, and shown that for all intents and purposes, taken on the world and won.

Jack Panos acknowledged his son's massive success, so much so that he awarded George the respect that he had so clearly craved. "My father's position with me is so mellow now, because ultimately he is pretty much overwhelmed by the power that I have managed to get for myself," George told the *Independent* some years later, in December 2005. "He has been really respectful to me for a long time, and, I think, quite remorseful about the way he was with me when I was younger." That meant more to George than anything—the fact that his father had finally accepted that his son was a talented musician who had made his own success in the world, just as he had.

A talented musician must make music and so it was back to the studio to work on his second solo album, *Listen Without Prejudice, Vol. 1*. This was to change quite a lot for George, deliberately on his part, of course, but right from the start it was clear to the rest of the world that he was determined to be seen differently. The title of the new album signified that, as did the attitude he brought to bear on his work. Just a few years earlier he had been willing to do practically anything to achieve fame, but this time around there were to be conditions and they were not at all what the executives at his record company wanted to hear.

Put simply, the album was to be released on George's terms and what that boiled down to was that there was going to be almost none of the traditional means of promoting it. It all came down to the fact that George wanted to be taken seriously now and he was neither going to tour to promote the album nor make videos to go with most of the singles. Had this been anyone of less stature, there is no conceivable way they would have got away with it, because what George was suggesting flew in the face of the received wisdom on how to launch an album. Such was the singer's clout at that moment that he was able to lay down the law on what he would and would not do and there was no one who could stop him. The label wanted his next record to come out just as much as George did: after all, he was not the only one making money on it. And so the latest phase of becoming a serious entertainer began.

After the massive commercial success of *Faith*, there were extremely high expectations surrounding this new album and in the longer run they were not to be fulfilled. Given George's refusal to play the game this is perhaps not entirely surprising, but it led to an extremely bitter rift with his record company that was to dominate the next few years and would ultimately mean that this was the last release of completely new material until *Patience* came out, a full fourteen years later. Indeed, George was on the verge of a new phase in his life: professional turmoil would join the personal. All the cards were shortly to be thrown up in the air.

This refusal to go out to promote the work he was doing was an early sign of the self-destructiveness that was to characterize the second half of George's life: he might have thought he was striking a blow for artistic integrity and the right of a musician to be judged on his music and not on his sun-kissed body and gold-streaked hair, but in reality he was sabotaging himself. With Andrew long gone from his professional life and no one with whom he shared a close friendship or significantly trusted on the scene with him, whatever the murmurings of record-industry executives, he was out on his own.

"At some point in your career, the situation between yourself and the camera reverses," he told the *Los Angeles Times* in 1990. "For a certain number of years, you court it and you need it, but ultimately, it needs you more and it's a bit like a relationship. The minute that happens, it turns you off... and it does feel like it is taking something from you. I would like to never step in front of a camera again." He did, of course, but from that moment on everything began to change. The über-sex-symbol status that *Faith* had given him began to slip away and, although this must have been in many ways a relief, it is hard for anyone to believe they are well and truly past their peak.

George's public anguish was so great that it attracted attention from an unexpected corner—Frank Sinatra, one of the most influential artists of the twentieth century. No one knew more about the vagaries of press coverage than Sinatra and he was so irritated by what he took to be George's self-pity, when he read an interview with him saying that fame had made him miserable in the *Los Angeles Times' Calendar* magazine, that he wrote an open letter in response. Dated September 9, 1990, it appeared the following week:

"Talent must not be wasted," the great man wrote. "Those who have it—and you obviously do or today's *Calendar* cover article would have been about Rudy Vallee —those who have talent must hug it, embrace it, nurture it and share it lest it be taken away from you as fast as it was loaned to you. The tragedy of fame is when no one shows up and you're singing to the cleaning lady in some empty joint that hasn't seen a paying customer since Saint Swithin's day. And you're nowhere near that; you're top dog on the top rung of a tall ladder called Stardom, which in Latin means thanks-to-the-fans who were there when it was lonely. Trust me. I've been there."

It is not known whether George ever saw the letter.

The release of singles from the new album began: as with *Faith*, there were a string of them, some performing better than others, all begging to be taken seriously.

The first was to be Michael's last ever US Number 1, "Praying For Time." Concerning social ills and injustice, it prompted the *Rolling Stone* critic James Hunter to call it, "a distraught look at the world's astounding woundedness. Michael offers the healing passage of time as the only balm for physical and emotional hunger, poverty, hypocrisy and hatred."

At least Hunter, like his fellow critics, enjoyed it. The single got into the Top 10 in the UK, the only one of five singles from the album to do so. It also had a video of sorts, which attracted attention mainly because it was like no other George Michael video. Directed by Michael Borofsky, it featured the lyrics of the song with a blue-and-black background that ultimately turns into the album's cover. Its sheer novelty value ensured repeated play on MTV.

The second UK single, released shortly afterward, was "Waiting For That Day," so closely influenced by the Rolling Stones' classic "You Can't Always Get What You Want" that the line itself appeared at the end of it and Mick Jagger and Keith Richards received co-writing credits. It didn't do very well, although the B-side, "Mother's Pride," did receive some attention, mainly because the first Iraq War (August 1990–February 1991) had begun and the song was about the sadness of conflict.

Next up, and the second single in the US, was something slightly different: a catchy pop song of the type George used to make, with all the attendant flamboyance, a real reminder of the good old days. But it was intensely autobiographical and if ever there was a song that George Michael had produced that was a clue to his inner turmoil, this was it. The song, far and away the best on the album and the one most people still remember, was "Freedom! '90" and just as Wham! tapped into the feel of the early 1980s quite brilliantly, George did so again now, although admittedly it was the accompanying video that was totally of the moment it portrayed. It was a meeting of fashion and pop, the perfect marriage of the two in fact, combining one of his best songs with a series of supermodel-dominated images that have lasted for years.

"Freedom! '90" was about a man who finds himself living a lie and is desperate to be true to himself. In retrospect it is incredible that its real message wasn't understood straight away: "I think there's something you should know / I think it's time I told you so... There's someone else I've got to be..."

Even at the time it was understood this was a cri de coeur that represented a real-life conflict with which George was struggling, but it was misinterpreted (in public, at least) as the agonized cry of a teeny-bop star who wanted to be taken seriously and later taken as a reference to the struggles the singer was going to have with his record company. In fact, of course, it was George desperately wanting to be able to come clean about the true nature of his sexuality and yet still, even now, being unable to do so, not least as *Faith* had turned him into more of a heterosexual sex symbol than ever (although he was working as hard as he could to overturn this).

It was the only other single on the album to get its own video, and that was ironic, too. George was still refusing to appear himself, and so he managed to line up the absolute top models of the day to lip sync the song. Linda Evangelista, Christy Turlington, Tatjana Patitz, Cindy Crawford and Naomi Campbell had just appeared together on the cover of the January 1990 issue of British *Vogue*, one of the most potent images of the supermodel era, and George secured the services of all five of them to mouth the words to his song. There were five male models there, too —John Pearson, Mario Sorrenti, Scott Benoit, Todo Segalla and Peter Formby—but they received nowhere near the same amount of attention. What this in effect meant was that a gay man's anguished desire to reveal the real person within was being revealed by a cast of beautiful women. Not, it must be said, that George would have objected to that in the slightest. Whatever the nature of anyone's sexuality, being associated with that level of glamor is never going to hurt.

The girls on the whole were keen. The only one to demur was Linda Evangelista, she who once famously proclaimed that she wouldn't get out of bed for less than $10,000 a day. "He thought it would make us into a big deal, that it would be good for us. I was like, 'Please, we're here. We've already arrived!'" she observed wryly. But George convinced her and, in the longer term, Evangelista was glad to have taken part: "Little did I know that to this day, when someone meets me for the first time, they bring up that video," she told *Vanity Fair* in 2015. "That's what they remember. So yeah, George was right."

The girls were paid $15,000 each (about $28,000 at today's values); the video was shot by David Fincher, who had previously worked on Madonna's "Express Yourself" and would go on to make quite a name for himself with a string of films including *Se7en*, *Fight Club*, *The Social Network* and *Gone Girl*. The video had a noir-ish feel, with some people detecting the influence of the recent science-fiction flick *Blade Runner* (1982). The clothes were styled by Camilla Nickerson, who went on to become a contributing editor for US *Vogue*, while makeup was done by Carol Brown. Each girl got a verse of her own to lipsync, while three items associated with *Faith*, namely a leather jacket, a Wurlitzer jukebox and a guitar, were shown during the three renditions of the chorus, each in turn being shot to flames. The symbolism was obvious. George was present for filming: "We'd drink red wine in the evenings because it kind of went on late, and George was just like one of the gang, in the trailers, hanging out," leading hairstylist Guido Palau recalled to *Allure* in Augusr 2015.

The video opens with a freshly blonde and bobbed Linda Evangelista looking about as stunning as it is possible for a person to look, hesitantly beginning to mouth the words of the song, while, somewhat incongruously, a kettle begins to boil in the background, presumably to make the supermodel's cup of tea. After that each supermodel gets her own scene and her own personality: alongside the stunning Evangelista, the two most memorable images were those of a naked Cindy Crawford writhing in a bath and Christy Turlington parading majestically through the shoot in a sixty-foot-long linen sheet. Filming took place over several days in Merton Park Studios, in South Wimbledon, London.

"My part was to make the girls the best they could look as who they were," Guido Palau told the *New York Times* (December 26, 2016). "They weren't playing characters. They were playing themselves. And each had their own personality: Linda the comedian, Christy much more classic, Cindy the pinup, Tatjana this kind of film noir, and Naomi a very strong kind of woman. We extracted that from them. They weren't prodded at all, though there were some surprises, like Linda's hair, which she'd done for a job for someone else. It wasn't like I said, 'Oh, dye your hair blond,' not at all. At the time, we really didn't realize how iconic the video would become. I was probably a bit naïve about the whole thing seeing how it was a bit of a lucky-break job for me."

"Iconic" barely begins to describe it. The video made a huge impact and the models remember it fondly, too. "I remember them sending me a Walkman so I could learn the words before I got to set," Cindy Crawford told *Harper's Bazaar* in October 2015. "The studio was huge and dark and smoky. Someone explained to me that my first shot would be in a bathtub. They oiled me up and put me in an empty tub with a smoke machine to look like steam. I had to sit on an apple crate because you couldn't see me over the edge of the tub. My second shot was sitting on a chair with a towel on my head and I kept thinking my part wasn't going to be that sexy... I think it stands the test of time and it still looks amazing today."

In the same article, Christy Turlington gave an insight into how the video was shot. "It was a whirlwind," she said. "I flew in from LA and drove straight to the set, so I was pretty delirious. Each of us filmed for a day on our own, except Linda and I overlapped on the last day because we had a scene together. They were long days. I don't recall any specific direction from David Fincher. He was focused on the lighting, I recall. George was there the whole time and very involved. I didn't get the cassette for the song until I arrived. I listened to the track repeatedly the entire drive to the studio. I barely had the lyrics down when we filmed. My first shot was me crawling behind a paper board with a slit cut in it so it only revealed a part of my face. Every time I couldn't remember the words, I ducked down so only my eyes were visible. By the end of the shoot, I couldn't not hear the song in my head."

Tatjana Patitz also enjoyed the shoot, telling *Harper's Bazaar*: "All the models and I knew George Michael—I think I had done a photo shoot with him at some point before. His manager contacted my agent to see if I could do the video. George wasn't in it—he wasn't even on the set when I was there... When I shot my segment it was just me on the sound stage in London, and it took all day for each girl. I was up against the wall in this leopard robe, and David told me to imagine that I was in this huge loft by myself, relaxing. He was very clear with his direction. The hairdresser did my hair really curly—I was like, are you trying to make me look like I put my fingers in a socket? And then he also had me lie on that chaise-lounge and smoke. But the way it came out, it looked so cool. When you're doing something, you don't know what it's going to look like, but the way they cut it together, with all the close-ups, is amazing. It was shot on film, which to me is so romantic. The digital world has become so crisp and unforgiving, but film is just... yummy!"

Naomi Campbell also has happy memories of the video. "I came to the set on the first day they were shooting," she told *Harper's Bazaar*. "Oh my god, it was crazy! It was during the fashion collections, so I came straight from Paris, and I'd done four or five shows the day before and we finished at two o'clock in the morning. They didn't have the Eurostar then, so I took the six o'clock train to London and then went to the airport. I didn't sleep—I went from the plane to the shower to the set. I was up all night working to work all night again! But it was great. I love George Michael, and I love all the girls who were in it, and the director, David Fincher, is a great filmmaker."

One of the male models was John Pearson. "My agent called up and said: "Hey, do you want to do this video? All the big girls are doing it,'" he told the *New York Times* in

December 2016. "Of course I said yes. I was a big George Michael fan. I used to see him all the time in London at the clubs. I arrived at the studios at three o'clock in the afternoon and met David Fincher briefly, and then basically sat around all day and watched while Christy and Linda were being shot. There's one shot where Linda puts her head underneath her sweater that's amazing. That wasn't rehearsed. Linda really knows how to use her body to communicate in an elegant way, never cheap and tawdry.

"George was there, very warm and nice but very shy... In the end, I was paid $15,000 for the day, which is not bad to hang out with these fabulous, beautiful girls... And it turned out to be one of those fabulously easy, surfing-the-day jobs, everyone riding on this wave of semi-stardom and recognition for the models. I really didn't realize how big it all was at the time."

No one realized how big it was going to be, not even George himself. But perhaps unsurprisingly, given the supermodel presence, the video and the fact that the song was far more upbeat than much of the rest of the album, it was a big hit. It got to Number 8 in the States. Although it only reached Number 28 in the UK, it charted well elsewhere in the world, getting a Number 1 slot in Canada, and if truth be told, it's probably fared much better than anything else from that disc. George sang it at the closing ceremony of the 2012 Olympics and the resonance was still there: it was to remain one of the favorite songs from that stage of his career.

At the time it was so successful that it even had an influence on the prevailing counterculture of the time. Candis Cayne is an actress known for her role in the American TV series *Dirty Sexy Money* (2007–09), who was in a New York-based drag act at the time. "There was a group of girls in NYC in the '90s, and we didn't want to model ourselves on anything other than the supermodels," she told the *New York Times* in the same piece that had quoted John Pearson. "Linda and Naomi and Christy. So when the video of 'Freedom!' came out and they were all in it, we were obsessed. I used to do shows at Boy Bar, so I decided I was going to do 'Freedom!' and got Lina and Mistress Formika and Sherry Vine to play the various parts. I was Linda. She was my favorite. We did the whole thing naked under white sheets. After the very last chorus, we dropped the sheets and were completely naked, holding our groin areas. That song meant a lot to us. There were singers we knew were gay then, but no one really talked about it." The real message of the song was clear to them, but as Cayne said, the climate was still not right to come out.

"Freedom! '90" was followed by two more releases, "Heal The Pain" and "Cowboys And Angels," the only single George released that didn't make it into the UK Top 40, and apart from "Freedom! '90," the reaction to the album was not what he had grown accustomed to. Some of the reviews had a downright respectful tone to them, mixed with a little regret. Everyone acknowledged that George wanted to grow up but the trouble was—he just wasn't as much fun as he used to be. "So no more breathless, pushy, addictive pop tunes like his '87 smash 'I Want Your Sex,' which made him a favorite video pinup," wrote Greg Sandow in *Entertainment Weekly*. "Instead he searches for his lost identity, writes a gentle antiwar number called 'Mother's Pride,' and sings an inward-turning, almost morose [Stevie] Wonder song, 'They Won't Go When I Go'... But all this carefully crafted understatement exacts its revenge: The album gets boring. *Faith* might have been pushy and brash, but it was amazingly vital, and much more fun. If *Listen Without Prejudice, Vol. 1*—polished, pretentiously titled, and, for all its noble sentiment, entirely unchallenging—is the best music the newly mature George Michael can give us, I'm going to mourn the insufferable brat he apparently thinks he used to be."

*Rolling Stone* was kinder: "This time around, George Michael has begun to think that he should provide something to his fans beyond fun and games. Fun and games at Michael's level needn't be underrated—as he sings on 'Freedom! '90,' such stratagems happened to yield a captivating sound for millions of people who like to listen to the radio," wrote James Hunter. "On this anxiously titled album, though, he's operating from the proposition that a damn good sound is only the starting point for how much pop music can achieve. If *Listen Without Prejudice* starts a trend among Michael's pop generation to move beyond image to integrity, it could make 'rock and roll TV' sound more consistently and convincingly like music."

Stephen Thomas Erlewine on allmusic.com reflected after the fact that it wasn't one of George's best: "George Michael's follow-up to the massive success of *Faith* found him turning inward, trying to gain critical acclaim as well as sales," he wrote. "*Listen Without Prejudice, Vol. 1* is not an entirely successful effort; Michael has cut back on the effortless hooks and melodies that crammed not only *Faith* but also his singles with Wham!, and his socially conscious lyrics tend to be heavy-handed. But the highlights—the light, Beatlesque harmonies of 'Heal the Pain,' the plodding number one 'Praying for Time,' and also 'Waiting for That Day' as well as the Top Ten 'Freedom'—make a case for his talents as a pop craftsman."

The jury was out on this next stage in George's career. The album didn't sell nearly as well as the previous; 8 million to *Faith*'s 28 million, and performed poorly in the States, although it fared much better in the UK. It garnered a Brit Award, winning Best British Album. But the high-risk strategy of no video and no tour was not paying off, not that George realized it yet: "It takes so much strength to say to your ego, 'You know what? You're going to keep me lonely, so I have to ignore you,'" he told the *Independent* in December 2005. "I realized those things my ego needed— fame and success—were going to make me terribly unhappy. So I had to walk away from America, and say goodbye to the biggest part of my career, because I knew otherwise my demons would get the better of me."

Of course that was said much later, with hindsight. But

it was true: George wanted to change his image and he succeeded. What he was not so happy about, however, was the fact that his second solo album wasn't the same smash as the first, and a little perversely, perhaps, given that it was he who had refused to do much promotion on its behalf, he chose to think that it was his record label's fault. In the meantime, however, he decided that he would do a tour after all and so, throughout 1991, he spent most of the year on the Cover to Cover Tour, taking in the UK, Brazil, Japan, Canada and the United States. In Brazil—of which more in the next chapter—he was reunited on stage with Andrew Ridgeley, who joined him for a few numbers during the encore at his performance at the Rock in Rio event at the Maracanã Stadium in Rio de Janeiro in January 1991.

This was emphatically not a tour to support *Listen Without Prejudice, Vol. 1*: rather, said George, it was about him singing his favorite songs. And he was true to his word: as well as singing some of his own hits, including "Everything She Wants," "I'm Your Man," "Careless Whisper" and "Freedom! '90," there were many other numbers made famous by different performers, including "Desperado," "I Believe (When I Fall In Love With You It Will Be Forever)," "Superstition," "What a Fool Believes" and more. It was as if one part of George knew he had to get out there and perform his new numbers, while another was stubbornly refusing to do so, hence throwing in so many other numbers as well.

He acquitted himself well: "George Michael may never

again reach the pinnacle of popularity he hit three years ago with his multi-million selling album, *Faith*," wrote Stephen Holden in the *New York Times* in October 1991. "But as a concert performer, he has certainly gained in poise and stamina since his last appearance in New York City. At Madison Square Garden, where his Cover to Cover tour opened a two-night stand on Friday evening, the 28-year-old English singer made a frisky master of revelries, singing and dancing his way through an ambitious program that interwove original songs with his interpretations of mostly well-known contemporary soul and funk hits by others."

Nestor Aparicio of the *Baltimore Sun* agreed: "When George Michael informed last night's crowd at the Capital Center that it was the final night of his American tour, expectations immediately rose," he wrote. "The question was, could he deliver enough enthusiasm and excitement even as the Cover to Cover tour was winding down with each minute? But much as he did in his American debut as a solo performer three years ago at the Cap Center, Michael delivered a most memorable performance." Indeed, it was memorable wherever he played, which was just as well: George was not to tour again for another fifteen years.

# SOMETIMES THE CLOTHES DO NOT MAKE THE MAN

# 8

# LOVE AND TRAGEDY

At the beginning of the 1990s, George Michael's life changed completely and it was now that the problems that were to overwhelm him in the years to come began to make their presence felt. He was never to have the sex-symbol image again that he had right up until the end of the *Faith* tour: that might have come as something of a relief to him, but equally it could have been a cause of some regret, because however conflicted he might have felt about public perception via private reality, very few people really object to being termed one of the most attractive people in the world. It has also been speculated upon in some quarters that it was that dichotomy that produced the work that it did. Great artists tend to be conflicted souls; inner peace is not generally the ideal creative breeding ground. All these inner torments would eventually destroy George but there may well also have been the impetus to create the work he did. There was to be more of course, but he was nearing the end of the glory years.

All of which makes it doubly tragic that in 1991 the potential for great happiness opened up before him and was quickly snatched away. Just when George had the opportunity to find the happiness he had been looking for with another man, the plague of the 1980s and 1990s reared its ugly head—AIDS. George had certainly been aware of the AIDS virus—everyone was in the 1980s, especially the gay community, which was suffering mightily from the disease.

George always maintained publicly that he had had straight relationships as well as gay ones and of course contracting HIV would have been a danger to the women involved, too, if the relationships had been fully sexual ones. But if Brooke Shields' account is anything to go by, this strongly suggests his girlfriends were close friends— maybe not much more. The other women involved have all maintained a discrete silence about the exact nature of what went on between them, but it speaks volumes that after George died in December 2016, Kathy Jeung posted an affectionate tweet about him that sounded very much as if she was talking about a friend: "Like my childhood with my dad and family, I spent some of the best times of my life with George—I can barely encompass in words what George means to me, I treasured our #specialfriendship— to just scratch the surface with no exaggeration, he was the most generous, hilarious, brilliant, talented, #truefriend."

Who knows? George did have female lovers but he was entering a stage of his life where women were friends, mothers, sisters and so on, but no more. His own version of events was as follows in conversation with the *Mirror* (June 2007): "Basically, I had three girlfriends [Brooke Shields, Pat Fernandes and Kathy Jeung] and all through that time I cruised as well. It only really used to happen when I was beating myself up about something else. I played around with the idea that I was bisexual—mostly by getting drunk. But then the HIV thing happened and I couldn't sleep with a woman without telling her that I'd slept with a man. Obviously my attraction to women was not strong enough to make that conversation worth having. So I started not sleeping with them at all." On another occasion, however, in an interview with *GQ* in October 2004, he said that Kathy Jeung had been his only bona fide girlfriend and that she knew he was bisexual.

In actual fact, George was sleeping with an awful lot of men. There was after-hours cruising in the clubs and bars catering to gay clientele; in gay circles almost everyone knew that George was gay and quite a few people he worked with knew him from the cruising scene, but they closed ranks around him because even at this late stage to come out would be a game-changer. And George was just not ready to take that irrevocable step. "I lost my nerve," he explained to the *Mirror* in June 2007, both of that period and of the earlier days with Wham! "I wanted to come out but I didn't realize how successful we were going to be. I think that's understandable. I was nearly 20 and we were the biggest band in Europe, and within two years the biggest pop band in America. If your goal is to become the biggest-selling artist in America, you're not going to make life difficult for yourself, are you?"

Ironically, of course, what he really did—and he later realized this—was to make life far more difficult for himself by creating tensions that would one day lead him to seek the oblivion of drugs. Those tensions were compounded by terrible personal loss. Meaningless anonymous sex is never going to bring anyone lasting happiness, and George was finally to meet the person with whom he had an emotional connection and with whom he could eventually find a deeper attachment that might, had circumstances been different, have resulted in a life-long tie.

It was during his Cover to Cover tour in 1991 that George met Anselmo Feleppa, the man who would become his first true love. Feleppa was a fashion designer and there are different accounts from George himself as to how they met: on one occasion he told the *Independent* he saw "a really cute guy" in the audience—"he was so distracting, I actually avoided that end of the stage." After the concert, Feleppa came to his dressing room (which would imply that while George might have avoided one part of the stage, he possibly got some kind of invitation to him) and that was that.

On Radio 4's *Desert Island Discs*, however, he told the story slightly differently: "I don't know if people will relate to this, but there have only been three times in my life that I've really fallen for anyone," he said. "And each time, on first sight, something has clicked in my head that told me I was going to know that person. And it happened with Anselmo across a [hotel] lobby. This was the first love of my entire life."

Whichever way it happened, George found love and in the early days was very happy. Anselmo Feleppa came from a mountain town called Petropolis, outside of Rio, but with the two of them equally smitten, he followed George back to LA, where he was to base himself for a time. George introduced him to friends; Anselmo was well liked by everyone and the stage should have been set for a happier and more stable phase of George's life.

For a while, it was a revelation and George talked about it in the slightly disbelieving tones familiar to anyone who has unexpectedly found love, whether they are gay, straight or somewhere in between. But in George's case it had the added dimension of allowing him to enjoy being who he really was. "It's very hard to be proud of your sexuality when it hasn't given you any joy, but once you have found somebody you really love, it's not so tough," George said to the *Huffington Post* in February 2009. Anselmo "broke down my Victorian restraint, and really showed me how to live, how to relax, how to enjoy life. I was shagging around but I had so little experience with men that my sex life was so ridiculously inadequate for me, right until I met Anselmo really... He was the first person I had ever loved, and I discovered he loved me too."

George was to stay faithful to Anselmo but the relation-ship was doomed by circumstances over which neither had any control. Anselmo had been aware that he should have himself checked out medically and early on in the relationship he got an HIV test. It came back positive, something he was initially reluctant to share with George, because of the sadness it would bring—but, of course, in the longer term he had to. And so just a few months after meeting Anselmo, George discovered his partner was HIV positive. At that stage, this almost certainly meant death. George himself was to prove negative and later stated that he always practiced safe sex. "There was no way I was having sex without a condom and there were only certain things I would do," he declared in an interview with *The Advocate* in January 1999. But his new partner had not been so fortunate. George now found himself in the position of taking care of Anselmo behind the scenes while Anselmo was suffering from a condition that was associated with the gay community, and at the same time still having to maintain a heterosexual image to the public at large. The stress must have been indescribable. Nor was this the full extent of the trauma in his life at the time.

George was still smarting over the disappointing reception of *Listen Without Prejudice*. It is one thing to decide to lower your profile, quite another when that results in people not buying your records, and with all the concern he must have been feeling about Anselmo on top of this, something inside him just snapped. In 1992 he launched a lawsuit against his record label, Sony, saying that he wanted out of his contract, according to the terms of which he was due to make a further six albums, on the grounds that the company hadn't supported his most recent album's release. Sony pointed out in response that George had refused to appear in promotional videos and that was what had really caused the problem. The battle would drag on for years, although it is worth noting that Sony maintained a scrupulous politeness in everything they said about George in public: whatever disappointments there had been about the record, George was still a mega-selling artist.

The case went to court in 1994 and it turned out that the roots of all this trauma actually lay in the Wham! days and the first contract George had signed with Innervision, a contract that he had needed help in getting out of, and a contract, he asserted, that had put him in a weak position to negotiate throughout his career. Through various convoluted twists and turns of his subsequent contracts, the situation, in the wake of the Wham! break-up, meant that George had to produce eight albums for Sony, two of which of course had already come out. (It was the same reason why Andrew Ridgeley had been required to make a record after the break-up of Wham!) George asserted that the contract he was in now tied him in for far too long, that it was a form of modern-day slavery and that the case he was bringing was not about money, given that he already had more than he knew what to do with, but about integrity. Sony was "a giant electronics corporation which appears to see artists as little more than software," he said. The record company did not retaliate in kind.

The case, which was a first of its kind and attracted huge amounts of attention because it not only involved superstar George Michael but had repercussions for other entertainers and their contracts, went on for years. The complexities of the arguments need not be gone into here, but suffice to say that George lost the case initially, appealed, and a form of compromise was eventually reached when, in 1995, Virgin in the UK and DreamWorks in the US got together to buy Sony out of their contract after George had point-blank refused to record for them again, whatever the outcome of the court case. Something was needed to break the impasse. Sony finally agreed to release the singer when they saw he was serious about not recording for them again, although they extracted a heavy price: the rights to a greatest-hits album, a share in profits from future albums and a £25 million lump sum from the two companies who were buying him out. Somewhat ironically, he would return to Sony ten years later.

One immediate upshot was that plans were shelved indefinitely for *Listen Without Prejudice, Vol. 2*, which was destined never to appear. George had written some new material for the album and instead he put the songs on something quite different—*Red Hot + Dance*, an album produced by the Red Hot Organisation, which was dedicated to raising funds and awareness to fight HIV/

AIDS, something clearly very much on George's mind at the time. Again all the clues about his sexuality were there if you cared to look at what was really going on in his life, although admittedly the project was also supported by some heterosexual artists, among them Madonna, Seal, Lisa Stansfield and Sly & the Family Stone. George played an active role in pulling the album together, working as a producer as well as contributing three original tracks.

One of the songs was "Too Funky," which was released as a single and clearly designed to replicate the success of "Freedom! '90," which it did not. Released in 1992 and his final single for Sony before the legal wrangling began— George was to donate the royalties to the AIDS awareness charities he was supporting elsewhere. It concerned sexuality and was none too subtle with it. "Hey, you're just too funky for me / I gotta get inside of you," were the first two lines, but the song never really developed from there.

The single featured Mrs Robinson's famous line in the 1967 film *The Graduate*: "I am not trying to seduce you... Would you like me to seduce you? Is that what you're trying to tell me?" It ended with another line from a rather different source—an episode of the Tony Hancock show called "The Radio Ham" in which the actress Annie Leake snaps, "Would you stop playing with that radio of yours? I'm trying to get some sleep."

In fairness it didn't do too badly, getting to No. 4 in the UK and becoming the most played record in Europe in 1992, and again the accompanying video centered on the fashion industry, but while the tone of the earlier video had been noir-ish, now it purported to be satirical and didn't really work. George was cast as a fashion photographer, snapping models on the catwalk, but instead of celebrating their beauty, there was a sense that fun was being made of it. It was a surprising take because some of the biggest names in the fashion world were involved: designer Thierry Mugler created the costumes and Jeff Beasley wrote the concept after attending one of Mugler's benefit fashion shows. Originally it was to feature the same five supermodels as "Freedom! '90," until Mugler decided he wanted a new line-up.

In the event only the über-fabulous Linda Evangelista was kept on from the original five: the other models were Eva Herzigova, Nadja Auermann, Emma Sjöberg, Estelle Hallyday, Shana Zadrick, Tyra Banks, Beverly Peele and Emma Balfour. Actresses Julie Newmar and Rossy de Palma, and the performance artists Joey Arias and Lypsinka were also to be found on the video. In the event, though, the magic of the first video was not recreated and although it performed respectably at the time in no way did it define the era as its predecessor had done.

There was another contribution to AIDS research when George performed in the Freddie Mercury Tribute concert on April 20, 1992. The Queen front man had recently died of AIDS and in his last-ever radio interview had praised *Faith*. One of the songs from the night, "Somebody To Love," went on the *Five Live* EP, which performed well commercially and also benefited AIDS research. There was an accompanying video, but George was apparently still in Greta Garbo mode and refused to appear.

From now on, George's energy and attention were to be taken up by his fight with Sony while a private tragedy was taking place outside of the limelight. Indeed, George later revealed that he thought his anger at Sony reflected the rage he felt at what was happening to Anselmo Feleppa, who was now slipping away. He eventually died of a brain haemorrhage in March 1993, on a visit to Brazil to see his family. George was in London at the time and learned of his death by a phone call. It was the news he had been dreading and he blamed himself.

"It was untimely, but that way he never lost his dignity, and I suppose I was spared the worst of what some people go through," George told GQ in October 2004. "But I'm still convinced that had he been in the USA or London, he would have survived, because just six months later everyone was on combination therapy... I think he went to Brazil because he feared what my fame would do to him and his family if he got treatment elsewhere. I was devastated by that. The idea that he had the opportunity to go somewhere better but wouldn't take it because of my fame makes me feel very guilty."

Of course it was not remotely George's fault: AIDS exacted a high toll in those years, but this immediate assumption of personal blame did not bode well for the future. Years of the strain of covering up the reality of his life—which he was still doing, but now with the added burden of a deceased lover whom he couldn't admit to—were taking their toll, the case with Sony too went on for years more, also extracting a heavy emotional price, and now the first person George had truly fallen in love with was gone. Anselmo had been able to do something more for him, not that either of them seemed to have realized that—plug an Andrew Ridgeley-shaped hole in George's life. While there had never been a physical relationship between George and Andrew, there had certainly been an emotional one. Curiously, George never seemed to make that connection himself.

At any rate, the loss devastated him. "Can you try to imagine being any lonelier than that?" he asked the *Independent* (December 2005). "Try to imagine that you fought with your own sexuality to the point that you've lost half your twenties. And you've finally found a real love, and six months in, it's devastated. In 1991, it was terrifying news. I thought I could have the disease too. I couldn't go through it with my family because I didn't know how to share it with them; they didn't know I was gay. I couldn't tell my closest friends, because Anselmo didn't want me to. So I'm standing on stage, paying tribute to one of my childhood idols who died of that disease... the isolation was just crazy."

Anselmo's death did, however, make George take one major step: the very next day he came out to his parents. Even if the public were to stay in the dark for a few more years, he was sick of pretending to be something he wasn't

Having met at school, Andrew Ridgeley and George Michael soon became world-famous as Wham! topped the charts.

*Above*: George with Bob Geldof and Bono during the final performance at Live Aid in 1985.

*Below*: Andrew and George on stage during Wham!'s farewell concert at Wembley Stadium in 1986.

On stage during the Faith World Tour – the success of George's debut solo album had sent his career to new heights.

*Above left*: George arriving at the High Court in London in 1993 during what was to be a turbulent decade for the singer.

*Above right*: Pictured with Naomi Campbell, who starred along with a host of supermodels in the iconic music video for 'Freedom! '90'.

*Below*: George with his beloved parents, Kyriacos and Lesley.

*Above*: Having had his sexuality revealed to the world in 1998, George remained in a relationship with Kenny Goss for over a decade.

*Below*: George performing with Sir Paul McCartney as part of the Live 8 benefit concert in London in 2005.

George performing to huge crowds in Dublin and Paris during the 25 Live Tour in 2006.

*Above left*: George addressing the media following his recovery from pneumonia in 2011.

*Above right*: Presenting Adele, an artist who had considered George a musical hero, with a BRIT Award in 2012.

*Below*: The stunning scene during the performance of 'Freedom! '90' at the Closing Ceremony of the 2012 London Olympics.

*Above*: George performing at the Royal Albert Hall during the Symphonica Tour in 2012.

*Below*: A selection of tributes left outside George's home in London following his tragic death on Christmas Day in 2016, recognising his legacy as a gay icon as well as a musician.

to his nearest and dearest and so took what some might see as a rather brave step—he did, after all, come from a traditional Greek Cypriot family and he had no way of knowing how they would react.

In the event, they took it well. George's mother was not only supportive but mortified that he had had to bear the burden on his own and for the rest of her life Lesley Panos tried as hard as she could to make it up to him. George's father Jack absolutely rose to the occasion, difficult as he might have found it, and, clearly determined not to replicate George's younger years, which the singer felt had been so marred by disapproval, gave his only son his total support. "He never displayed any disappointment or homophobia," George told *GQ* much later, in October 2004. "I'm sure he felt it, and it was hard for him, but he didn't lay any of it onto me, which I have to thank him for. This is sad, but I do feel success can negate a parent's disappointment. I genuinely feel that although his son is gay and not going to give him any grandkids, my dad's consolation is that I have done well in life."

That was one burden off his shoulders at least, but what with all the stress and loss in the background and the ongoing fact that AIDS remained a preoccupation for the gay community, a lot of the pressure remained simply because the fear of AIDS was still present. "I had an absolute rubbish level of sex through that whole terror, between 1985 and 1994—with the exception of the sex I had when I was faithful to my first real partner, Anselmo,"

George said later, as reported in the *Mirror* in June 2007. But Anselmo was gone now and life had to be faced once more.

In later years, George became not only a lot more open about his personal life, but a lot more self-reflective. That made it all the more surprising that while acknowledging completely the importance of their relationship, he never seemed to realize that, pre-Anselmo, it was former bandmate Andrew Ridgeley who had for many years provided him with the emotional security that he now craved. The closest relationships are not always the sexual ones. He was often asked whether there had been a homoerotic element to their friendship, but while the answer was no, it never seemed to occur to him quite how important the affection had been – much more important, certainly, than the passing physical encounters he had in the hundreds, which were ultimately, perhaps, quite meaningless. And he was even able to joke about the fact that at school, people sometimes suspected that it was the snappy dresser Andrew who was actually gay.

"Andrew loved camp clothes," George recalled to the *Mirror*. "He'd go to school in cherry silk trousers and have three little Adam Ant braids. Everyone spent their time going: 'Is he gay?' And I'd go: 'He's really not!' He was beautiful but not in a way that was going to attract me. He was too pretty, too feminine, too elegant. I can understand everyone thinking we were sleeping together—but he loves women." Neither Andrew nor Anselmo were present in George's day-to-day life. It was a theme he was to return to. "I can't think of anything more vile than sleeping with Andrew," he told *GQ* in October 2004. "I've known him since he was 11 and he's one of my best friends. There probably was something homoerotic there, simply because we were so close. But luckily, I never fancied him. Also, he's just not my type, to be honest. Beautiful though."

In the wake of Anselmo's death, George plunged into a mire of grief and depression and it was then that the bad habits began that were to cause him so many problems in the future. His use of cannabis began to escalate, reaching, by his own admission, its height at twenty-five spliffs a day, and a sense of aimlessness and desolation set in. He wasn't working, because of the issues with Sony, and deprived of a purpose filled his days with getting stoned and little else. Over and again, George was to seek help for his addictions, but at this stage he clearly had no idea what a dangerous path he was on. And it was at this point in his life that a rather unlikely friendship began: one with Diana, Princess of Wales. In many ways it was two lost souls seeking each other, but it appears that George and Diana could, had he wished it, have become more than just friends.

"I was invited to the Palace many, many times before I actually met with her because I was so afraid of the publicity if we did become friends," he told the *Huffington Post* in February 2009. "And when we did meet, I think we clicked in a way that was a little bit intangible, and it probably had more to do with our upbringing than anything else. She was very like a lot of women that have been attracted to me in my life because they see something non-threatening. Maybe because I take care of my sisters and I'm so protective of my sisters, women seem to smell that. So women who had a hard time growing up or feel that they were not... you know... when I was still sleeping with women, my God it was absolutely all of the time. There were certain things that happened that made it clear she was very attracted to me. There was no question... I knew it would have been a disastrous thing to do.

"I was very upset when I saw the *Panorama* documentary [when Diana discussed her marital problems in public for the first time with Martin Bashir, aired on November 20, 1995], because she really didn't seem well at the time. It did really upset me because I thought people saw her at her most vulnerable... and I kind of feel guilty because she did really like me as a person, and I tended to shy away from calling her because I thought she must have so many people calling her for all the wrong reasons. I knew she was so suspicious of people by then, so I would almost treat her the way I know some people treat me. I would presume it was an intrusion to call, when actually you know they're lonely and would love to hear a friendly voice."

But no one needed to hear a friendly voice more than George. He was to find it again, in the longest relationship of his life, but even then his happiness was not unalloyed. More tragedy lay in wait.

# LOVE AND TRAGEDY

# 9

# COMING OUT
# (PART ONE)

The death of Anselmo Feleppa plunged George into a deep depression indeed and in some ways, it was to blight him for the rest of his life. Already he had been intent on lowering his profile and now, not for the last time in his life, he began to display distinctly reclusive tendencies, avoiding public appearances and, as the battle with Sony wore on, not doing much career-wise, either. It was a recipe for disaster. George had never in his life been idle: from the moment Wham! sprang onto the scene he was constantly planning his next move, working out his next strategy and above all writing songs. Now his days were spent in a fug of cannabis smoke, with neither his career to sustain him nor a close companion to give him emotional support. If you have nothing to get out of bed for, then the temptation is not to get out of bed.

If George had tackled his demons then, would it have been possible to draw back from the path that would lead him to his death, decades prematurely? It is impossible to say, but he had embarked on a road that was utterly destructive, and it was going to get an awful lot worse. At that stage, however, he slowly began to find himself again and one upshot of this was the song "Jesus To A Child." He had spent fully eighteen months unable to compose anything, but as he himself put it later, the song came to him in an hour, signifying that he was able to tap into his creative side once more. An extremely melancholic lament to a dead lover, it was inspired by the memory of Anselmo.

George performed his new song for the first time in public at the MTV Europe Music Awards show in 1994. It would be released as a single and would appear on the album *Older* a couple of years later, after the record company dispute had been resolved and he had found his new homes. The accompanying video was full of pictures of pain and suffering; while the outside world did not know the exact circumstances of what George had been through, it was obvious that he had had an extremely traumatic loss. After he fully came out in 1998 George was to dedicate this song to Anselmo whenever he sang it but at the time this was not the case, for to have done so would have also resulted in outing himself, something he was clearly not ready to do. It might have been an open secret in showbiz circles that George was gay, but the wider public hadn't been let in on the knowledge. But there were certainly no more female names being bandied about in connection with George; he obviously didn't have a girlfriend and didn't appear to be coming round to having one any time soon.

The song, when eventually released in 1996, was George's first self-written single to be released in the US and UK for nearly four years. Straight into the charts at Number 1 in the UK and Number 7 in the US, it presented a more mature and more reflective George. It was generally considered to be a more elegiac melody and, at around seven minutes, considerably longer than much of his previous output: "'Jesus to a Child' is among the most haunting of Michael's ballads, and one whose meaning could only fully emerge after his coming out," wrote *Slant* magazine in an article reprinted in December 2016, after George's death. "A slow-motion flamenco cry, written following the death of his lover, Anselmo Feleppa, 'Jesus to a Child' still remains supernaturally clear-eyed about what it means to love and to lose."

It was around now that George's appearance started to change. He was getting older, of course, and this was reflected in the title of his next album, but there was more to it than that. His hair was getting shorter; a buzz cut, now, rather than those lustrous golden locks that had turned him into such a global sex symbol. His wardrobe was changing too, with the denim look exchanged for much more leather. The designer stubble was carefully shaped and appeared for a spell in the form of a handlebar moustache. How much more of a hint would people need?

He was beginning to look, as he himself put it, more gay: it was as if he wanted to tell the world who he really was and if he couldn't do so openly, then he was going to drop as many hints as he could.

"The way my image changed in Europe was that I looked very different, I had very short hair—I had really a kind of gay look in a way," he told talk-show host Oprah Winfrey in May 2004. "I think I was trying to tell people I was okay with it, I just really didn't want to share it with journalists. The album I made in the middle nineties called *Older* was a tribute to Anselmo, really; there was a dedication to him on the album and fairly obvious male references. To my fans and the people that were really listening, I felt like I was trying to come out with them."

But it wasn't obvious to everyone yet, no matter how many clues George dropped. In later years he sounded almost exasperated: "By the time I actually outed myself I had tried every way to let people know that I was OK with being gay, even the fuckin' handlebar moustache for a little bit," he told the *Guardian* years later, in December 2005. "I didn't deny any of the stuff that came out in the newspapers. I just didn't say the three words. They can have the bloody moustache, they can have the pictures in the paper of my ex-boyfriend, but they can't have the three words, 'I am gay' or 'I love cock,' one of the two." But he clearly still felt some kind of pressure not to come out completely, even if that pressure was by now building up to such an extent that he was about to out himself in the most spectacular way.

The aura around him had changed, too. In the Wham! days he exuded youth, happiness and energy. Now there was a melancholy that hadn't been there previously, again an almost inevitability after suffering a great loss but all the more difficult to bear when you can't be open about it. And while when he did produce a song it tended to be a good one, he wasn't producing that many songs. When George went solo a truly sensational future had been predicted for him, but now there was a slight sense that he wasn't living up to his potential. The battle with Sony hadn't helped matters of course, but the internal conflicts that had done so much to produce such good music in the past now appeared to be subsuming him. And nothing in George's life would ever be on an entirely even keel again.

Matters did appear to be looking up in 1996, however, which was the year that George started releasing records again and also when he met Kenny Goss. Kenny was to be his longest relationship by far and after George died there was talk that they had been thinking of getting back together again, but back then he brought much-needed cheer to the singer's life. Kenny, a good-natured Texan from Dallas, had previously worked as a flight attendant, cheerleader coach and sportswear executive; he was to end up as an art dealer and the two had a variety of homes around the globe.

When George finally came out and started talking about his relationships, he initially said that he and Kenny met at Fred Segal, a department store in Los Angeles, but later confessed it had actually been in a spa – a highly respectable spa. "We thought if we told the truth, certain people would think we met cruising each other!" he told *GQ*. "But that wasn't what happened at all. We just got chatting and I asked him out for dinner. I wasn't even sure if he was gay."

But Kenny was gay and, more to the point, was as interested in George as George was in him. And then, in a breathtakingly awful act of fate, George's newfound happiness was dashed almost as soon as it was raised. He rang his mother to tell her that he had found a new companion, only to learn that she was suffering from cancer. "So I didn't even get one day to feel happy about having met Kenny," he told *GQ* in October 2004. "I was back into the black hole. I haven't had any dark days for a long time now, but there was a point when that was all I had. I just used to sleep and sleep. Some days I could barely put one foot in front of the other; it was real depression. I was on Prozac. It made a slight difference, but for it to have really worked I would have had to be pumped so full of drugs I think the side effects would have been dreadful. I was so close to the edge all the time that I kept getting knocked back into the abyss, constantly looking over my shoulder wondering where the next blow would come from."

Of course there was a history of depression in the family and it is widely accepted that there can be a genetic link. In retrospect, George acknowledged that Kenny quite possibly saved his life. George's maternal grandfather and uncle had both committed suicide, the latter by horrible coincidence on the day George was born. And despite the presence of Kenny, the depression was not going to disappear from George's life anytime soon—years later he said that he had been in a bad way for twelve years, which meant that he'd effectively spent his twenties struggling with his sexuality and his thirties wrestling with the "Black Dog" as Winston Churchill aptly described it. It might explain his destructive drug use. Fate really did seem to be dealing him a bad hand at that time. George believed that it was essential to have an operation on his back or risk paralysis; it left him with rods in his back and in permanent pain. His dog too was getting older and so he bought a new puppy to console him against the older dog's eventual death: the puppy drowned in the Thames and then the older dog died anyway. It was a nightmarish time.

He coped, as much as he could. In 1996, the album *Older* came out, featuring a very different-looking George on the cover—moustache, goatee, air of menace—and such was the excitement surrounding a new George Michael record that despite his absence from the charts for years it went straight into the No. 1 slot in the UK album charts, although it was to receive a more muted reaction in the US. It also produced six top three singles over the next two years, a remarkable achievement, especially given what was going on in George's personal life, and creating a record that has not been broken to this day.

After "Jesus To A Child," there was "Fastlove," which

earned George his third Ivor Novello Award for the most performed work in 1996 (the other two being "Careless Whisper" in 1985 and "Faith" in 1989; he also won three "Ivors" for Songwriter of the Year in 1985, 1989 and 1996), "Spinning The Wheel" (which was kept off the No. 1 slot in the UK by the Spice Girls' debut "Wannabe"), "Older"/"I Can't Make You Love Me" (the latter was in fact on *Listen Without Prejudice, Vol. 1*), which was the worst-performing of them all—perhaps the public didn't want to see George as older—"Star People" (kept off the top slot in the UK by Gary Barlow's "Love Won't Wait"), "You Have Been Loved" and "The Strangest Thing," which was kept off the top slot by Elton John's "Candle In The Wind," which Elton had rewritten and re-released following the death of Diana, Princess of Wales. "You Have Been Loved" was also a tribute to Anselmo Feleppa, though it wasn't widely acknowledged back then.

Although the public loved the album and bought it in droves in Europe and the UK, the reviews were mixed. It wasn't exactly what critics were expecting and while everyone knew that George wanted to be taken seriously as an artist, some thought it was just too gloomy. The record had a considerably darker tone to it, employing a more jazzy sound, and it was as if the critics weren't entirely sure what to think.

"'Thank you for waiting,' George Michael writes on the back of his first studio album in almost six years. If anyone is really still waiting, they'll discover Michael hasn't lost his talent for writing pop songs as contagious as the Ebola virus, if only slightly more cheery," wrote *Rolling Stone* in February 1998. "Like the comedy director in the 1941 film *Sullivan's Travels* who wants to make 'serious' films, Michael desperately craves respect, not content with simply being an accomplished writer of silly loathe songs about relationships gone bad. Although he occasionally sounds like the Prozac queen Elizabeth Wurtzel singing 'It's My Party' in an empty karaoke bar, for those who can get past Michael's pretentious melancholy, *Older* is a surprisingly enjoyable record."

But Allmusic didn't think so: "*Older* is the album that many observers initially believed *Listen Without Prejudice, Vol. 1* to be—a relentlessly serious affair, George Michael's bid for artistic credibility. It's an album that makes *Listen Without Prejudice* sound like *Faith*. Michael has dispensed with the catchy, frothy dance-pop numbers that brought him fame, concentrating on stately, pretentious ballads—even 'Fastlove,' the album's one dance track, lacks the carefree spark of his earlier work. Although Michael's skills as a pop craftsman still shine through, his earnestness sinks the album. It is one thing to be mature and another to be boring."

*Entertainment Weekly* didn't like it either and was bang on the money about what was really going on behind the scenes: "The goateed man with the matted, severe Caesar haircut who stares at us from the cover of *Older* shows a hint of a smile with the faintest of confidence; half his face is hidden in shadows. He looks like Mephistopheles as pickup artist. Before you've even heard a note, the photograph announces that the George Michael we once knew is gone —although, based on *Older*, it's much more difficult to determine just who he has become. Something happened to Michael at the dawn of the decade, and whatever it is, he can't shake it."

The record still enjoyed huge sales—so much so that it was reissued in December 1997 as a "box package" including two discs: the original and another disc entitled *Upper*. The public attitude towards George was changing: he was obviously no longer the teenybopper of yesteryear, but he was turning into someone who was held, if anything, in even greater affection. There was a sense that he was deeply troubled, but equally an almost palpable desire on the part of the public for him to be all right. Many of George's fans had grown up with him; they had bopped along to Wham! and were now finding that his more mature music was describing their own life experiences.

The music industry was rooting for him, too. In 1996 George was voted Best British Male at the MTV Europe Awards and the Brits, Songwriter of the Year at the Ivor Novello Awards (and, the following year, Best British Male at the Brits), and he performed a full-length concert, his first in years, for MTV Unplugged. His mother Lesley was in the audience; sadly, a year later cancer claimed her life.

George plunged straight back into the most terrible depression and, as mentioned earlier, later credited his new partner Kenny for quite literally saving his life. There was that history of suicide in his family and as in all such situations, an unspoken fear among the survivors that it might happen again. Kenny was crucial to George at that stage: already on the road to serious drug addiction, having lost two of the most important people in his life within just a couple of years of each other and far more vulnerable than he had appeared when he was younger, George was entertaining some very black thoughts. Having just had his first album out in years, he lost the ability to write again, such was his despair, and friends became increasingly concerned as he sank back into the morass.

But at least Kenny was there. "If he hadn't been around, I think my life would have been in danger, in terms of me," George told GQ years later (October 2004). "After Mum's death in 1997, when I couldn't write and I felt really worthless, I don't think I could have taken it really. I think I might have been one of those cowards who choose a nasty way out. I don't know for sure, but I would imagine it would have been a very strong possibility if I hadn't had someone as strong as Kenny to rely on. He was there to put his arms around me and remind me there was something positive going on. I was never without stress from the moment I found out about Mum's cancer, but Kenny waited and he finally got to see me healthy and happy last year. Hopefully it was worth the wait."

One particular problem was that, as with Anselmo Feleppa, he blamed himself. This time around, though, it seemed as if he thought he was attracting negative karma and that this was some kind of spiritual retribution for turning his back on his career. It was nonsense, of course, but it is not unusual for family members to feel they are somehow at fault if something happens to a loved one; it taps into all the deepest fears in a person's psyche, especially if the loved one is still relatively young.

"I thought it was punishment because I turned round at the end of *Faith* and said, 'You know what? I'm going insane, and I know there's another way to do this,'" he told the *Guardian* in December 2005. "I thought, is it because I wasn't grateful enough for my talents? In terms of coming close to saying I don't want to live, that would have been after my Mum died. I had this overwhelming feeling that the best was behind me. I so loved my mum, and respected her. I'd have to be mentally seriously disturbed to even consider suicide because of what it would do to the people who were already devastated from losing my mother— my sisters and my father." But it didn't stop him from engaging in behaviour that was becoming dangerously self-destructive.

The worst thing George was doing to himself was the smoking of the spliffs, of which there were a daily and enormous number. Then again he was following in a long and centuries-old tradition, albeit an extremely harmful one: the artist who believes mind-altering substances contribute to their creative output. George certainly didn't understand what he was doing to himself in the early days:

"No, it was quite inspiring," he said, as noted in the same *Guardian* piece. "The album that resulted from it, *Older*, was the most creative I'd made at the time. Unfortunately, it is a writing tool now, which is one of the things that makes it hard to give up."

Of course he was deluding himself and a part of him knew it. In his interview with *GQ* in October 2004, he was asked if his smoking was linked to his depression: "If you've smoked it for a long time—which I have—it can be linked to depression, but I don't think that's the case with me. I'm sure it's bad for me in some ways, but I love smoking. I wish to God I didn't, especially as a singer. It was the most stupid thing I ever did, but I'm definitely a more together and happier man. In other words, I seem to have progressed mentally, regardless of being a pothead... But I wouldn't recommend it to the young."

It was destroying him, but George clearly didn't realize that. More than that: as well as allowing him to become far too dependent on something noxious, his drug of choice involved heavy smoking, which for a singer who needs to protect his lungs and voice is an absolute disaster. After the last few years he'd had, with even a new puppy dying, George clearly felt he needed a crutch, and even the happiness he'd found with his new partner couldn't contain the fears overtaking him. He was terrified of something happening to Kenny, who had given him the stability he needed and craved: "My biggest problem in life is fear of more loss," he continued. "I fear Kenny's death far more than my own. I don't want to outlive him. I'd rather have a short life and not have to go through being torn apart again. Kenny has to travel a lot with his job and we have fights before he flies because I try and get him to avoid British Airways or American Airlines in case he falls victim to a terrorist attack. When he leaves me, I panic. I can't relax until he's called to say he's arrived safely. But when I fly, I don't care and get straight on BA."

However, despite the fact that this had deepened into an extremely serious relationship, unlike in his relationship with Anselmo Feleppa, George was not being faithful to Kenny. He was taking risks—big risks, given every newspaper on the planet would have paid a fortune for the final confirmation that George Michael was indeed gay— and he was also displaying a kind of inner restlessness that hinted at a deeply unsettled state of mind. He didn't see it like that, of course. As far as he was concerned he was cruising again and why not?

"Some gay men manage monogamy forever, and I envy them because it's a great thing," he told *GQ* in October 2004. "But when you first meet someone, that chemical flows through your body and says 'fuck, fuck, fuck,' it's wondrous. If you can keep hold of that, great. But for me to experience that again in a relationship, I'd have to split with Kenny. When I walk into a restaurant I check out the women before the men, because they're more glamorous. If I wasn't with Kenny, I would have sex with women, no question. But I would never be able to have a relationship with a woman because I'd feel like a fake. I regard sexuality as being about who you pair off with, and I wouldn't pair off with a woman and stay with her. Emotionally, I'm definitely a gay man."

One who might still have been in some kind of denial, by the sound of it. And one who continued to be recognized everywhere he went, which may or may not have had something to do with the next major event in George's life to make the headlines. "I once tried a disguise," he explained in the GQ interview. "It was when I had longer hair and I tucked it up in a baseball hat and wore my prescription glasses. I looked nothing like me, or so I thought. But within a few minutes of leaving the house, someone said, 'Hello George, I didn't know you wore specs.' So I gave up on that."

Which was another way of saying there was absolutely no way that George Michael could go around the planet without being recognized. Most big stars are in a similar position and adopt all manner of survival strategies to protect themselves in a public place but, as George was getting increasingly desperate to stop living a lie, and after all this time in the public eye show the rest of the world who he really was, he was becoming more and more cavalier about being recognized. And this was to lead directly to his first, very public, arrest.

# 1 0

# COMING OUT
# (PART TWO)

In many ways it was astonishing that it took until April 7, 1998 for the truth about George Michael's sexuality to come out. As he himself had made plain, he'd dropped as many hints as he possibly could without actually issuing a press release that he was gay and it doesn't take a psychologist to work out that when he finally did come out, he had managed to engineer a situation in which he had no choice but to tell the truth. He was patently tired of the secrecy, tired that he couldn't acknowledge Kenny Goss publicly as his partner, and tired that he couldn't be honest about his real life.

And so it was that Lt Edward T. Kreins of the Beverly Hills Police Department was called upon to announce that George Michael, now thirty-four, had been arrested by a plainclothes officer who had "observed Mr Michael engaged in a lewd act" just before 5 p.m. on a Tuesday afternoon in a public lavatory at the Will Rogers Memorial Park, just across the road from the Beverly Hills Hotel, on Beverly Drive and Sunset Boulevard. The exact nature of the "lewd act" was not elaborated on but it wasn't hard to guess: George was alone and, apparently, could be seen by anyone walking into the rest room.

Officers from the Crime Suppression Unit had been making a routine check following recent complaints about lewd behaviour; George posted $500 bail and was released after about three hours. "It's not something you'd expect up there," said Lt Kreins with admirable sang froid. "It's pretty much a park where you'd relax, read a book and get some wedding photos taken." George pleaded "no contest," was ordered to undergo counselling, fined $810 and sentenced to eighty hours of community service and that was it. With a leap, he was free.

Unsurprisingly, the news made headlines around the world (one newspaper memorably advized him to "Zip me up before you go-go"), while the park authorities, deeply embarrassed, discovered that the Will Rogers and Greystone parks were listed on websites that detailed cruising opportunities. There was a flurry of activity: the park authorities warned potential cruisers to stay away while various gay-rights groups objected that they were being unfairly targeted, but for George the short-term embarrassment was massively outweighed by the fact that the deed was done and now, at long last, he could be himself.

In fairness, it took a little while. While George might have been subconsciously setting himself up, he was at the time humiliated and went underground, disappearing from the public eye for a number of weeks. Over in London, the Capital FM London Awards ceremony was taking place and attendees were asked what they thought: "I am sad for him because I think he's a great artist and it's a shame when you get tainted in any way," said Errol Brown of Hot Chocolate, while actor Paul Barber, who played the character of Horse in *The Full Monty*, said: "I'm a fan of his, and it won't stop me playing his music. George Michael is the business, he's great." The portentous tone of the comments might seem strange today but that was the way it was in April 1998, the era before civil partnerships, let alone gay marriage. Homosexuality, especially when it came to light like this, was still viewed in some circles as askance. Times were changing but not quite that fast.

It was not until later that year that George gave his version of events and by that time he was keen to make a joke of it. "I got followed into the restroom and then this cop—I didn't know it was a cop, obviously—he started playing this game, which I think is called, 'I'll show you mine, you show me yours, and then when you show me yours, I'm going to nick you,'" he told MTV. "Actually, what happened was once he got an eyeful, he walked past me, straight past me and out, and I thought, that's kind of odd. I thought, maybe he's just not impressed. And then I went to walk back to my car, and as I got back to the car, I was arrested on the street. If someone's waving their genitalia at you, you don't automatically assume that they're an officer of the law. I've never been able to turn down a free meal."

That last was the first public hint that not only had this not been a one-off but that George Michael was far more promiscuous than most people realized until then. Indeed, in the wake of George's death in 2016, the journalist Piers Morgan revealed that the singer had confessed to about 500 lovers in the space of seven years. But what had also — obviously—not been commonly understood until then was that George was in fact in a long-term relationship and that Kenny Goss might not be best pleased by this turn of events (it was George's compulsive cruising that would lead to a rift down the road). "I'm not saying that I have an open relationship with my boyfriend but he knows who I am," George continued to MTV in November 1998. "He knows that I'm generally oversexed, so he's been very, very good. We love each other and he understands that it was a stupid mistake and he's forgiven me, I hope."

George also hinted that he thought some elements of the press might have had something to do with it. They had been desperate to share what was by now a fairly open secret and this certainly gave them the opportunity to do so. "I don't think it was by chance that this happened to me," he said, although he was almost certainly allowing a more paranoid side to emerge for it has never been proven anywhere that the British press has any kind of link to the LA police. "We have some fairly vicious people in the country where I come from and they work in certain streets in London. I think it might have had something to do with it. There was a little more cooperation than you would expect between the police and the paparazzi."

At any rate, he protested, he thought that everyone had worked it out by that time anyway. "I really thought to my fans I outed myself with the last album because—and it wouldn't seem that way in America because in America there hasn't been that much publicity about me in the last seven or eight years because I just haven't been here or been on TV—but, actually, there's been a lot of publicity about my sexuality over the years in Europe and my ex-partner's death was reported very widely, so when I dedicated the album to him and wrote the album for him, I felt like I was coming out to my fans, and I didn't really care about people who weren't interested in my music," he added.

"So, I certainly wasn't gonna go to Fleet Street and say, 'Yes, I'm gay.' The main point is that I outed myself in my life about eight or nine years ago and I've been out with everyone in my life—even casual acquaintances, my family, friends—anyone who's met me within that time has known that I'm gay, just not the press. So, really, this doesn't feel like an outing, this is just public outing. But any gay person who comes out realizes that the tough bit is your friends and family and that was a great thing—it was a great, liberating thing and I did it a long time ago. I don't know if I would have come out to the press. They would have got me, some way or other. This is how it ended up because I wouldn't give it to them."

It was rather a sour view, but understandable under the circumstances, given the way some elements of the press had covered it, something alluded to after George's death by Andrew Ridgeley, backed by George's fans. But George was certainly able to turn it to his own advantage, and quickly as well. In October 1998 he released a new single, "Outside," about the joys of al-fresco gratification, which satirized the whole incident, the singer claiming he'd service the community ("But I already have, you see!"). The video was even more marked: directed by Vaughan Arnell and filmed in June that year, just a few months after the incident happened, it starts off as if it was some kind of European porn film complete with a few real (female) porn stars with a short Swedish monologue before the main action begins. This showed a police helicopter hovering over LA, monitoring all types of sexual activity, gay and straight, with George, dressed in an LAPD police uniform, dancing with his backing troupe in a public loo got up to look like a nightclub. It ends with numerous arrests.

The consensus was that George had handled matters rather well, not least as the single sold well in the UK, peaking at Number 2, a sure sign that the public still loved him, whatever his private peccadilloes might be. By openly poking fun at himself he calmed some of the more hysterical commentary; by addressing the issue with some honesty he had, in the modern parlance, taken back ownership of what had happened. The same did not quite hold true in the more puritanical US, however, and George was never to find the success there again he had enjoyed with *Faith*. And this was LA, so there were further repercussions: the police officer who arrested George, Marcelo Rodriguez, sued for $10 million on the grounds of emotional distress. It bobbed around in the courts until 2006, when he was told that as a public official, he could not legally recover such damages.

Ellen Aragon, Deputy District Attorney at the Beverly Hills District Attorney's office, was actually quite sympathetic, while maintaining that George had to understand he had really done something wrong. "[The video] could, in context, be quite humorous—without seeing it, it's hard to know how to take it or what to say about it. I would just hope that it doesn't reflect an attitude on his part that the whole thing is simply a lark," she said on November 5, 1998, according to MTV News, following that channel's airing of a live interview with George Michael. "It's not the kind of thing that we think he should be going around wearing a hairshirt and beating his chest about, and it's not as tasteless as making fun of a serious crime like a murder. Nevertheless, I think that the citizens of Beverly Hills don't appreciate their children playing in parks and possibly walking in on men exposing their erect penises to other men, so in terms of our community, we consider it an offense." In the event, the video was considered innocuous enough—George was poking fun at himself more than anything else.

One of the great sadnesses of George Michael's life is

that, once finally out and open with the world about his sexuality, he did not go on to find the happiness and peace of mind he so clearly sought. Whether this inability to find peace was rooted in his childhood or the years of covering up, it is impossible to say, but this was certainly not to be his last arrest – there was more to come, both on another public sex charge and also connected to drugs. And it was his drug usage that was to lead him into trouble time and again: George just did not seem able to understand what a catastrophic effect it would have on his health. But the sense of loss and bereavement was to stay with him; there was a spiritual sorrow that all the casual sex and drugs in the world would not be able to heal. But at least now there was nothing to hide.

Until the LA episode, George had not really spoken publicly about being gay; now he seemed to find it hard to shut up. All those years of censoring himself gave way to the polar opposite: he wanted to talk about it; he was going to talk about it, no more secrets and total honesty. It didn't take long for him to come to the reasonable conclusion that he had probably subconsciously decided what he was going to do and it wasn't just about coming out; it was a reaction to the various crises that had seemed to be crowding into his life.

"Now, I honestly think it was a desperate attempt to make the trauma in my life about me, because then, maybe, I could control the outcome," he told GQ in an interview in October 2004. "Up to then, the traumas had been out of my control and the outcome always bad. From the point when Anselmo got sick, I felt out of control. There were also family problems too hurtful to talk about, but I was snowed under with things I couldn't do anything about. So I gave myself this six-month distraction from every day being about missing my mother. For six months, I had to work hard to fight for my career, but once that was done there was nothing to stop what came after it, which was just total depression. But as subconscious plans go, it was pretty successful." According to the *Guardian*, he had stopped cruising, though—"It's one thing to get caught cruising and make a joke of it and turn it around, it's another thing to get caught again and look stupid, isn't it? And anyway it's not any fun any more because I outed myself. That was the whole point"—although ultimately George was to take it up again and indeed get caught once more.

There was also the minor matter of George's female fans. He had accrued quite a few of them in the early days and many had stayed with him throughout the years, growing up alongside him and appreciating him as a more mature artist. Posters of the singer had been pinned up on a lot of bedroom walls; he had been a lot of people's first crush and he clearly didn't want everyone who had been in that position to think he had been deceiving them. While he might not have been exactly straight per se, he had been a little confused. "I do want people to know that the songs that I wrote when I was with women were really about women, and the songs that I've written since have been, fairly obviously, about men," he told CNN in April 1998. "So I think in terms of my work I've never been reticent in terms of defining my sexuality. I write about my life, and I want people to know, especially people who love the earlier stuff, if they were young girls at the time, whatever, there was no bullshit there, you know?" In the UK, certainly, there was no obvious backlash about any of this; his former teeny-bop fans did not queue up to denounce him. There was a good deal of sympathy from many quarters as people understood that the strain of the secrecy had been a further burden to an already troubled man.

One irony was that George now faced criticism from another direction: the gay community itself, some portions of which seemed to feel he'd left it pretty late to come out and only did so when he had to. In 2005, a documentary was made about his life called *George Michael: A Different Story* (it was the one in which he said that Andrew Ridgeley was far happier than he, George, could ever be). In it, Boy George was highly critical of George's decision to make a video about his experience in California, and also said that he took himself too seriously. George did not take it well and appeared to think that the real problem was that he had also had relationships with women.

"How can a gay man not think that video was a good thing?" he snapped to the *Guardian*. "He doesn't even realize how homophobic he sounds. Someone like [Boy] George will not accept that anyone has any form of bisexuality. It's always just a cover-up, dyouknowwhadImean? He does the same things as straight people do. He wants to know he can tell. And for anybody to judge a man or woman for not coming out when they don't know their family situation... unless that person is doing something actively hypocritical to the detriment of the gay community, then shut the fuck up, you know nothing, youknowwhadimean?"

George was also adamant that he was not going to "tone down" his sexuality to please anyone else. "You only have to turn on the television to see the whole of British society being comforted by gay men who are so clearly gay and so obviously sexually unthreatening," he told the *Guardian*. "Gay people in the media are doing what makes straight people comfortable, and automatically my response to that is to say I'm a dirty filthy fucker and if you can't deal with it, you can't deal with it... I'm just very regular. Haha! I feel I should have extreme tastes but I don't. I'm very much what gay people call vanilla, but I am filthy in that I want it a lot! I have always practiced safe sex." And then came a rather surprising admission: "Deep down, part of me thinks the wrath of God is the reality. I don't believe that for a moment, but when I was younger it was hard not to feel that way as a gay man." The little Greek Cypriot boy was clearly still there, underneath it all.

The other uncomfortable reality was that George was now occasionally subjected to homophobic abuse. If people wanted to be unpleasant to him, it was the work of a moment to start talking about public lavatories, a subject also used to put him down. George became more assertive and strident about the subject, not less, and in the years to come seemed to go out of his way to shock. In another interview with the *Guardian*, a newspaper he clearly liked, in 2009, he talked about cruising, a pastime he had clearly taken up again: "The handful of times a year it's bloody warm enough, I'll do it. I'll do it on a nice summer evening. Quite often there are campfires up there [on Hampstead Heath, near his home]. It's a much nicer place to get some quick and honest sex than standing in a bar, E'd off your tits, shouting at somebody and hoping they want the same thing as you do in bed."

On a typical evening, he continued, he would, "Maybe eat locally, hang out, and then probably go off and have a shag or have someone come here and have a shag. It's not typical—that's probably a couple times a week... If it was shagging with Kenny, I wouldn't have to invite him round, would I? Kenny gets his, believe me."

For all the bravado that didn't sound too much like a man completely satisfied with life, but George was a complex creature who was never going to be categorized. But at least there was the music. Back in 1998, just after it all kicked off, he was not just working on "Outside:" his last contractual obligation to Sony was a greatest-hits album and *Ladies & Gentlemen: The Best of George Michael* duly came out, complete with the single "Outside." The collection was divided between two discs: one, the ballads, "For The Heart," and the other, the dance music, "For The Feet." It went straight to Number 1 in the UK charts, where it stayed for eight weeks, becoming George's most successful album in the UK and, at the time of writing, selling around 15 million copies.

The critics loved it. "When George Michael was riding high on the charts, only a handful of critics acknowledged that he was a brilliant mainstream pop singer/songwriter who, at his best, rivaled his idol Elton John in crafting state-of-the-art pop songs and productions," wrote Stephen Thomas Erlewine on allmusic.com. "As a solo male hitmaker, virtually nobody could touch him between 1984 and 1994, and even when his grasp began to slip, he still made compelling music... the collection is a monster, as impressive for its size as it is for its achievements. To some casual listeners, the sheer scope of the collection may seem overwhelming, since it doesn't just have the hits, but also rarities, compilation tracks, lesser-known singles, and duets."

A second single from the album was released, a cover of Stevie Wonder's "As," which George sang as a duet with Mary J. Blige. It was not on the US version of the disc, however, amid rumors that Mary's record company president would not allow it because he didn't approve of the association with George Michael. It was a reminder that for all George's openness and honesty, there was a reason he had kept quiet in the first place.

As the twentieth century drew to a close, George had a rare missfire: *Songs From The Last Century* was an album of cover songs released on Virgin. It did poorly in the

States, managing to ascend only to 157 on *Billboard*, and although it fared a lot better in the UK, it became George's only solo album not to reach Number 1. The numbers included "Brother, Can You Spare A Dime?," "My Baby Just Cares For Me," "Miss Sarajevo" and "Roxanne," for which George shot a video filmed in the red-light district of Amsterdam. There was also an alternative version of "Brother, Can You Spare A Dime?" filmed when George duetted with the great Italian tenor Luciano Pavarotti in one of the latter's *Pavarotti and Friends* series, which appears on George's second album of greatest hits.

No one seemed to know quite what to make of it. George changed direction several times in his career and no one doubted the quality of his voice, but it wasn't clear why such a modern artist would adapt the persona of an old-school crooner at such a young age. Just as Bob Dylan has turned to Frank Sinatra covers in the latest phase of his career, George Michael was looking back on the great American songbook, as it were. Perhaps it was a natural outgrowth of his writer's block. Whatever it was, it failed to excite. "After *Older*, could this be Coffin Dodgin?" asked *NME* cruelly (September 2005). "The progression in Mr Michael's career has been a little confusing of late. His last album failed to produce the great songwriting moments, but his forcible outing by the LAPD saw him salvage some persecuted minority kudos. 'Outside,' plus video, was funny and vital, so it's strange that he should decide to sleepwalk out of the '90s dressed in borrowed pyjamas."

George responded with silence. He appeared to be approaching the end creatively, or was at the least mired in an uninspired lull: and while there would be another studio album down the road, a live album after that, the big single was behind him. He withdrew, lay low for long periods, only to emerge, blinking, back into the headlines, for all the wrong reasons. He was a giant in the industry and remained so until his death but there was the distinct feeling that his heart wasn't in it any more.

# THE PROTEST
# SINGER

The start of the new millennium saw nothing like the frenzied work rate from George Michael that had existed in the early years, but fans had had some time to get used to the idea that they would not be hearing so often from their hero. His relationship with Kenny Goss kept him in a fairly stable place, but the air of melancholy that surrounded him was not blowing away. George seemed to be deliberately avoiding any form of publicity. He spent most of his time in Goring-on-Thames, considering it his main home, and became an oft-sighted figure at the nearby Miller of Mansfield hotel. A small circle of friends visited, including Shirlie and Martin Kemp, who had known him from the very beginning, his agent Connie Filippello and lawyer Tony Russell. When he was in London he eschewed celebrity hot spots; George appeared to be actively pursuing a very quiet life.

But he was still working, sporadically, at least. In 2000, he got together with another massively troubled singer, Whitney Houston, who also died prematurely (at forty-eight) due to drug issues, to sing the duet "If I Told You That." The male voice was to have been Michael Jackson but it never came off and Whitney originally recorded the song as a solo before George's voice was added in. She was to perform the song in concert but George did not; they never sang it live together. It appeared on her greatest-hits album but not his. They recorded a video set in a nightclub together and the song was a hit.

Critical reaction was mixed. "Whatever magic might be found in this effort most certainly is going to come from the fine vocal performances," said *Billboard*. "Houston scats and offers shout-outs that give 'If I Told You That' a spontaneity and energy [...], while Michael still stands tall as one of the finer soul men to step in front of the mic. This pairing is mightily inspired... the track's instrumental palette is definitely of the moment, with a driving shuffle beat and layered vocals. The hook is catchy enough, with a chorus that's simple and easy to sing along with."

J. D. Considine of the *Baltimore Sun* opined that Whitney was "faking attraction with George Michael..." *LA Weekly* wrote "on paper, the Houston-Michael coupling is inspired. But Michael simply adds his pinched, nasal vocals to the track [...], the result of which is two people singing at one another and daring the listener to care."

After that there was silence for a full two years, before a short-lived frenzy of activity. In 2002, the single "Freeek!" appeared, the first of six singles from the forthcoming album *Patience*, although that was not to see the light of day in 2004. It was a big success in the UK and around Europe, propelling George to Number 1 country's such as Spain and Italy. The accompanying video, which cost £1 million to make, referenced science fiction, specifically *Blade Runner*, and was peopled with cyborgs and future technology, George in a rubber fetish suit, an orgy and women on leashes. There were rumors that the singer was hoping it would be banned, in order to maximize publicity. Although it did quite well in mainland Europe, it was a bit of a dud in Britain. "I just don't think 'Freeek!' was his best song," said Elton John. "But it's ok—we've all made those kind of records."

Perhaps it was disappointment to the reaction to "Freeek!" that made George decide to go out on a limb because he soon found himself at the center of controversy again. Finally, it was his music that did it and not his extra-curricular activities. The year 2002 was a tense one politically: after the terrible September 11 terrorist attacks, it had become increasingly clear that Britain and the US were preparing to attack Iraq and a fierce anti-war feeling was developing.

George might have seemed an unlikely protest singer but in some ways that is how he started out. The very earliest Wham! songs were about social issues and so, almost twenty years to the day after the release of "Wham Rap!," a song all about unemployment, he took on another issue of the day, in this case the impending war. The song was "Shoot The Dog" and it was to provoke a massive outcry, quite out of proportion to the impact the actual record made. George certainly got himself noticed with this one and was accused of everything from dabbling in politics that he did not understand to anti-Americanism. It is true that his star had already faded in the United States after the Los Angeles incident and never rose very high again, which may well have made him more reckless about upsetting Americans—but as he himself pointed out, his long-term partner was a Texan and he had spent long periods living in the States himself. At any rate he pulled no punches in what he did next.

If truth be told the lyrics were not his best, but in the line "They're gonna shoot the dog" his intention was clear: the dog in question, at least in parts of the accompanying video, was Tony Blair, with the British Prime Minister portrayed as President George W. Bush's poodle, although there were a few other canines in there as well. The video was in the form of a cartoon and given who it was taking aim at, seemed determined to cause as much offence as possible: George enters the White House via a men's loo; President Bush throws a ball for Tony Blair to catch, poodle-style; George goes to Iraq, steps on a missile, rides it, Dr Strangelove-style, into Cherie Blair's bedroom; Bush goes on to crawl into the bed; the Queen and Prince Charles get dragged into it; George seduces Cherie... and so it went on. For a protest against the upcoming war, it was difficult to tell if the bad taste was deliberate or whether everyone involved had simply taken leave of their senses.

Some people liked it—in the wake of his death in 2016, some cited it as George's best-ever video. George himself lost no time in proclaiming how serious he considered the matter to be, addressing the British Prime Minister in July 2002 through the *Daily Mirror* thus: "On an issue as enormous as the possible bombing of Iraq, how can you represent us when you haven't asked us what we think? Could we have a little chat about Saddam? 'Shoot The Dog' is intended as a piece of political satire, no more, no less, and I hope that it will make people laugh and dance, and think a little. I don't consider Americans bullies, but I do consider the American government bullying. Our government needs to reassure [our] Islamic population that we are not going into the Middle East with a gung-ho attitude, blindly following America."

He felt the need to elucidate further: "'Shoot The Dog' is simply my attempt to contribute to the public debate that I feel should be taking place regarding Iraq and Saddam Hussein... my intentions are genuinely to do something, however small, to protect all of us, the people I love, and the people you love, from a disaster we have the power to avoid." And elsewhere: "This is the most political thing I've ever done, and it's a massive and totally unnecessary risk for me. I know this is dangerous territory. But I feel this is such a serious time for us all that being silent is not an option."

He wasn't wrong about the risk he was taking. "It's either really ballsy or commercial suicide," Conor McNicholas, then incoming editor of *NME* said at the time. "The potential to have people burning CDs in the States and banning him from shops in the Bible Belt is very real. There's obviously a huge tradition of politics in rock music, but it's utterly died out and it's bizarre that it takes someone who was so manufactured to be the person who nails their colors to the mast." (That last was a little unfair —George was not a manufactured pop star but neither was he anyone's idea of a conventional protest singer.)

And Anna-Louise Weatherley, acting editor of *Smash Hits*, said that since the Los Angeles incident, "I think it's given him the courage to voice his opinions; he doesn't seem to be scared any more about how he's perceived."

However, there was the predicted furor. George's relations with the press had been a lot trickier since that LA incident, especially the more boisterous elements of the tabloid press. When it emerged that he wasn't planning on releasing the single in the United States, the *Sun* ran the story under the headline "COWARD"— "He's scared to release it in the States in case it offends those fans he still has left. What a cop-out"—forcing George onto the defensive.

He posted a message on his website:

The record was never intended for American release for the precise reason that I felt it could be misread in this very way, and it makes me truly sad that this press statement has been necessary. The song and video in question is definitely not an attempt to express anti-American sentiment, nor an attempt to condone the actions of Al-Qaeda.

I have lived with an American citizen for the past six years, and have had a home there for the past 10. And I would never knowingly disrespect the feelings of a nation, which has suffered so much loss, so recently, for any reason.

Shoot the Dog is simply my attempt to contribute to the public debate that I feel should be taking place regarding Iraq and Saddam Hussein.

I have tried to convey my message with humor, because the public is rightfully scared of these issues, and humor has often been a useful aide to political debate.

And believe me, however irreverent I may be of Mr. Blair and Mr. Bush, my intentions are genuinely to do something, however small, to protect all of us, the people I love, and the people you love, from a disaster that we have the power to avoid.

The record was never intended for American release, for the precise reason that I felt it could be misread in this very way, and it makes me truly sad that this press statement has been necessary.

Once again, no offence to Americans was intended, but politicians are humans, not gods, and God knows there has never been a more important time to remember that than now.

Sincerely, George Michael

The fact that George was to be entirely vindicated by history was neither here nor there. The *New York Post* called it a "tawdry tune." It was written that was a "past his prime pop pervert." George went on to CNN to explain that the song was anti-Blair, not anti-Bush: "This was absolutely an attack on Tony Blair, principally, and the perspective which is really predominant in Europe right now that he's not questioning enough of Mr. Bush's policies. It's anti-Mr. Blair and anti-Mr. Blair's reluctance to challenge Mr Bush. It's not anti-American in any sense. Satire is used for political purposes all the time, but obviously there's a time and a place. I think in the current climate, it can be very difficult to speak your mind, but sometimes, I believe, we're all in danger and I think this discussion needs to be widened."

Not that he was receiving that much support from his fellow musicians. Noel Gallagher, then at the height of his fame with Oasis, was unimpressed: "What's he trying to say? He's now trying to make social comment, this is the guy who hid who he actually was from the public for 20 years, now, all of a sudden, he's got something to say about the way of the world. I find it laughable. That's even before you get to the song, which is diabolical." Unfair, perhaps, but one of a number of criticisms now routinely levelled at

George for not coming out sooner. Whatever he did on this particular issue somehow landed him in the wrong.

The bickering got so bad that on July 12, 2002 George went on to ITV1's *Tonight With Trevor McDonald*, where he said that much of the criticism was down to homophobia. "It's been very heavily inferred that I was actually an Al-Qaeda sympathizer, that somehow I thought that there was something not horrific and shocking and undeserved about the attacks on September the eleventh," he said, going on to talk about the number of newspaper interviews he was doing to try to contain the fall-out. "I was trying to do some damage control because my life was in danger. Americans are very reactionary right now and I—because of that article —cannot return to America, even though my partner lives there. I love my home there, I love Kenny's family; I spend time, sometimes, in Dallas and sometimes in LA.

"I did release a statement anticipating a misreading of the video to try and make people understand that I'm not anti-American in any sense." And referring to some of the criticisms, which seemed to center on his sexuality just as much as his political opinion, he continued, "I don't think that there's any real connection between what I'm saying and the fact that I'm a gay man. But there's a lot of connection in the press as to those two things. For some reason I don't have a right to talk about anything because I got caught four years ago with a police officer in a Los Angeles toilet. Somehow that eradicates all possibility that what I'm saying might be for the best or is worthy of being discussed. I can't fight that kind of homophobia here and now. I think that it might continue. I think I might be up for much worse homophobia."

He also denied that this was a publicity stunt in the wake of "Freeek!:" "This would be the most stupid publicity stunt anyone ever pulled," he said. "I mean, look at the publicity I've got out of it. I'm not stupid—I knew I was going to walk into a wall of criticism because these are very reactionary times, but they're also very urgent times and I felt that I had to do this. I don't have any regrets about releasing this song. I think maybe I regret not somehow, you know, prepping it more in America because I released my statement to America on the same morning that the *New York Post* printed the first article. I wish I'd somehow gone there and said it is not an attack on American people who I have a great deal of respect for and if I had done that then maybe I wouldn't have to be here today."

All the publicity certainly didn't help record sales: the single only made it to No. 12, which was actually a lower chart position than "Freeek!" had achieved. Perhaps to accentuate the fact that his opinion of the upcoming war was heartfelt—and George was far from being alone in this—in February 2003, he recorded another protest song, a cover of Don McLean's "The Grave," originally about the Vietnam War, which he performed on a number of television programmes, including *Top Of The Pops*, his first appearance on the BBC show since 1986. That was not without controversy either: George wanted to wear a

T-shirt proclaiming "No war, Blair out" and claimed he was prevented from doing so by the BBC. He was "very upset," his spokeswoman said, adding that he had been told that his band, which was wearing the same T-shirt, would be edited out of the footage as they didn't have a change of clothes.

The BBC hit back: "We are not giving George Michael a platform to air his political views, we are giving viewers the fantastic opportunity to see an international star perform on *TOTP* for the first time in 17 years," it said in a statement. "George wore a black sweatshirt with denim jacket during rehearsals and a brown leather jacket and black hooded top during his main performance. At no stage did he wear a T-shirt. His backing singers did wear anti-war T-shirts but the programme was still being edited right up until transmission. The BBC has a duty to air all points of view equally, so if for instance, there was a pro-war song performed by an equally established artist it would be considered in the same way adhering to BBC editorial policy guidelines."

Don McLean himself, however, was very supportive: "I am proud of George Michael for standing up for life and sanity," he said in a message on his website. "I am delighted that he chose a song of mine to express these feelings. We must remember that the Wizard is really a cowardly old man hiding behind a curtain with a loud microphone. It takes courage and a song to pull the curtain open and expose him. Good Luck George. Don McLean, March

1st 2003."(Quoted on the artist's official website, www. donmclean.com.)

Toward the end of 2003, slightly to the bemusement of those who had watched George's bitter battle to extricate himself from his contract with Sony, the singer returned to the recording giant for what was to be his last blast of creative output. Sony had been careful never to badmouth him, not even at the height of their dispute, and now released a generous statement to mark his return: "We are delighted to be working again with one of the greatest recording artists this country has ever produced, who has made another classic album," Sony Music UK chairman/ CEO Rob Stringer was quoted as saying. And the move did make sense. For a start, Sony did actually own most of George's back catalogue, while secondly, it had escaped no one's notice that since leaving the label, George's career had lost some of its lustre. Low profile: good; low record sales: not so much.

His decision appeared to be vindicated almost immediately. In March 2004, George released his fifth and final studio album, entitled *Patience*. At the time it was thought of as a comeback record, as it was his first album composed of original material since 1996; instead it was his last hurrah. More was to come and George was to stay active creatively until his death, but this was the last of the kind of work and success that had taken him from the relative obscurity of North London to the heights of international stardom.

The album was to spawn six singles, two of them being "Freeek!" and "Shoot The Dog," which had already come out on the Polydor label. There followed "Amazing," "Flawless (Go To The City)," "Round Here" and, finally, "John and Elvis Are Dead," although that last was only sold as an Internet download. George himself seemed to realize it was an ending of sorts: he announced that this was to be the last album he made that sold through record shops and that all the music he made in the future would be available for free as a download: "I'm sure it's unprecedented, it's definitely unprecedented for someone who still sells records," he told Jo Whiley on BBC Radio 1 on March 10 of that year. "I've been very well remunerated for my talents over the years so I really don't need the public's money. It does two things—it takes the pressure off to have a collection of songs every so many years, which is what nearly killed me. I'm not pretending I won't be famous any more, but in the modern world if you take yourself out of the financial aspect of things, you're not making anybody any money, you're not losing anybody any money. Believe me, I'll be of very little interest to the press in a certain number of years. I'll hopefully be a happier man, giving my music and also doing something really positive with my music if people are generous enough to donate to the site. I'll remove myself from all that negativity."

Poor George was deluding himself if he thought he would no longer be of interest to anyone and, in retrospect, while the sentiment looked extremely generous, it also opened the door to the final era of his life, of which more shortly, which was totally dominated by headlines about alcohol, drugs, arrests and all manner of problems. Had he kept himself in the mainstream of the music industry it might have given some structure to his life. Instead a certain aimlessness would cloud the coming years. He was already forty, disillusioned and unhappy, and it is hard to know what could have saved him now. The album was still darker than anything before it: it contained the song "My Mother Had A Brother," referring to George's gay uncle who had so tragically killed himself. Another song, "Please Send Me Someone," was about Anselmo Feleppa's death. The upbeat Wham! days seemed a lifetime behind him.

The fans, ready to welcome George back into their midst, were delighted and the album was a massive success, however. It went straight in at Number 1 in the UK (and No. 2 in Australia), sold over 275,000 copies in the first week and became one of the top-selling albums in the year (2004). That success was not quite replicated in the US, where it was released without "Patience Pt 2" and "Shoot The Dog" and launched with an appearance by George on *The Oprah Winfrey Show*, in which he showed the talk-show host around the surprisingly unostentatious interior of his country home. It got up to No. 12 on the charts.

Despite the commercial success, the reviews were mixed. "Michael used to be one of pop's punchiest singles artists, but you wouldn't know it from this undistinguished downer," wrote Nicholas Fonseca in *Entertainment Weekly*. "Baring your tortured soul is one thing, but unleashing a barrage of self-pitying ballads and expecting people to listen is a test of even the most open-minded fan's patience."

Sal Cinquemani on *Slant* magazine was none too impressed either: "If there was ever a time for George Michael to get his groove back, it's now," he wrote. "Now, in 2004, he's thanking us for our Patience (or, possibly, asking us to have a bit more of it), but *Patience*, his first original studio album in eight years, is a mixed bag that can be somewhat of a downer."

Alexis Petridis in the *Guardian* tried to be kind but had his reservations: "*Patience* tries to do too many things at once: express unimaginable personal grief, set the world to rights, snarl at the media, and hymn a new love, Texan boyfriend Kenny Goss," he wrote. "At 70 minutes, *Patience* is too long. Had Michael lost its weaker moments, its impact would have been greater."

But George's heart wasn't in it any more. Too many personal tragedies allied to the struggle with his sexuality compounded by the pressure he felt to go on producing great work proved to be too much. Sometimes success when you are still so young can cast a shadow: no matter how good the music he simply could not replicate the verve and happiness of the Wham! days when he and Andrew Ridgeley were still young and had everything to play for. George was approaching the musical end.

# 1 2

# A MUCH-
# LOVED MAN

A nd so, slowly but surely, the career of one of the greatest
singer-songwriters of his generation began to wind
down to a close. George Michael had got everything he
could possibly have wanted in those far-off days when he
was a plump little boy with spectacles, dreaming of being a
pop star—fame, wealth, respect—but it had done nothing
to make him happy. In retrospect it appears quite clear that
he never was happy after the break from Andrew Ridgeley.
The sun was beginning to set on a truly astonishing career.

In 2005, George appeared at the Live 8 concert in
London's Hyde Park, singing with Paul McCartney on
the Beatles' classic "Drive My Car;" the following year he
released *Twenty Five*, his second greatest-hits album in two
formats: CD and a three-CD limited edition. The former
contained four songs from the Wham! days, a number of

new songs, including duets with Sugababe Mutya Buena ("This Is Not Real Love") and Paul McCartney ("Heal The Pain"); the limited-edition three-CD version contained fourteen lesser-known tracks, among them a Wham! song and a new song, "Understand." It went straight in at Number 1 in the UK and No. 23 in the US; the three discs were entitled *For Loving, For Living* and, for the limited-edition third disc, *For The Loyal*.

This one got excellent reviews, full, as it was, with many songs that had by that time stood the test of time—twenty-five years of it, to be precise. "George Michael's music is as important for its universality as it is for its sexual specificity," said Popmatters. "Presumably, 'Amazing' is a love song about Michael and his partner, yet its genderless pronouns translate to all kinds of relationships. Rather gracefully, George Michael has proclaimed his love for men without alienating his fans. What *Twenty Five* illuminates that *Ladies & Gentlemen* did not is how Michael has come full circle in making peace with his sexuality."

Allmusic.com wrote that, "*Twenty Five* celebrates George Michael's 25 years in the recording industry by presenting a near-perfect collection of highlights from both Wham! and his solo career. For fans, having 'Everything She Wants,' 'Careless Whisper,' and 'Wake Me Up Before You Go-Go' on the same collection as 'Faith,' 'Father Figure,' and 'Freedom! '90' is reason enough to pick this up."

That was the year that a documentary was made about George's life: *George Michael: A Different Story*, the documentary in which he made it plain that Andrew Ridgeley's life was so preferable to his own. Andrew appeared on it and it became extremely clear what a huge toll the split between the two of them had taken on George's life. "We couldn't really see how we could take the concept that was Wham! into adulthood," said Andrew. "And we were right."

Possibly so, but it is tragic they didn't find some way of continuing to work together and it was now clear that Andrew had been the impetus behind the rift: he had had enough. Footage of their last-ever concert was shown and, as they embraced in front of the screaming fans, it was George who was hanging onto Andrew, giving every impression that he didn't want to let go, as Andrew clapped him reassuringly on the back. Nonetheless, Andrew felt the solemnity of the occasion too: both their lives were about to change. "I didn't enjoy it as much as other shows, because that whole period leading up to it was a difficult one for me," he recalled. "I kept thinking, you know, when it's over, when the encore's done, that's it. And that was a really difficult concept to get to grips with."

"He was tired of being taken potshots at as the lucky guy who's coasted along with George Michael," said George, meanwhile. "He was so much more than that. If I was about to go to the place that I believed I was going to go to there was no way that we could hang out in the way that we had always done. There was just no way. It would have been too difficult for Andrew. So I understood our relationship was going to have to reach some different kind of level. That was tough. And I had no idea how much I was going to miss that support, how close to lunacy I would feel without that support."

It is not too fanciful to say that Andrew Ridgeley was the real love of George's life. There was never any physical relationship between them and the emotional bond was one of friends, brothers even, not lovers. But the most important person in someone's life is not always their romantic interest: it is the person with whom they share the deepest bond. The bond between George and Andrew is evident in that documentary; George never found anyone else to whom he was as close.

But he did have Kenny Goss. By this time, civil partnerships had been brought into the UK for gay couples. A precursor of gay marriage, they were designed to ensure that gay couples had all the legal rights and protections in terms of property, pensions and so on as those accorded to straight couples, and George went on the record as saying that this was something he and Kenny would do once civil partnerships came into effect from December 21, 2005. In the event, the two didn't go ahead with it: wealthy in their own right, they didn't need the financial protection, but many gay couples wanted a partnership for the symbolism of being able to show their commitment to one another.

Rumors were rife that the ceremony had been called off because George did not seem to be able to stop himself from cruising for sex, but this was hotly denied by the man himself. He phoned in to Richard Madeley and Judy Finnigan's Channel 4 show—he was friendly with the presenters—to deny reports of a liaison on Hampstead Heath and used the occasion to say that the ceremony had been postponed on the back of press intrusion, not any extracurricular activities on his part. "With all the rubbish I've had to put up with in the last six months, we wouldn't get a small private wedding, which is what we want," he said. "I wanted something small and quiet, but I don't even think we'd get away with that at the moment." In actual fact, the ceremony never took place.

In the meantime, George embarked on his first major UK and European tour in fifteen years, proving that he still had it and the fans still loved him. In June 2007 he became the first artist to play live at the newly done-up Wembley Stadium, where he was fined £130,000 for playing thirteen minutes longer than he was supposed to. Celebrity guests included former Spice Girl Geri Halliwell, actress Claire Sweeney, presenter June Sarpong and Ivana Trump, the first wife of Donald Trump.

It was an "amazing honor," said George. "I have felt a huge association with Wembley from when I was a child."

Behind the scenes, however, all was not rosy, as things were truly beginning to unravel.

Nevertheless, George seemed willing to try something new. He appeared on *Eli Stone*, an American comedy/ drama about a San Francisco lawyer played by Jonny Lee

Miller who has an inoperable brain aneurism that leads him to hallucinate (and which might also mean he is a prophet). The creator of the show, Greg Berlanti, was a big fan of George's and each episode of the first series was named after one of his songs. In fact, the series was dominated by the musician—in the first episode, Eli starts to hear "Faith" everywhere (in a hallucination). It culminates in seeing George sing the song in his sitting room.

George agreed to appear in four of the episodes, as a guardian angel, including the premiere, "Heal The Pain" and "I Want Your Sex," in which he steps out of the hallucinations and into reality. He plays himself, self-deprecatingly, too, when one of the other characters confuses him with U2's Bono. ("Happens all the time," says George, removing wraparound sunglasses. "But I had the glasses first.") The latter episode concerned a girl who played the song over her school's PA system to complain about the school's abstinence-only sex-education policy and gets suspended for her efforts. His last appearance on the show, the season's finale, "Soul Free," saw him perform "Feeling Good," one of the most uplifting scenes in the drama. *Eli Stone* only lasted for two seasons and has been largely forgotten, but it was an indication that George was prepared to branch out.

Greg Berlanti was devastated when he heard George had died: "I've only witnessed true genius a few times in my life," he tweeted when he heard the news. "One of those was watching George Michael lay down 'Feeling Good' for *Eli Stone*'s 13th episode, 'Soul Free' in which the singer, appearing as a God-like figure, led what was eventually a group performance of the aforementioned tune. He was an incredible talent and even more a sweet, kind man to all lucky enough to work with or spend time around him. May he rest in peace."

Those appearances in *Eli Stone* actually put George back on the map as far as the United States was concerned. He also made an appearance on the 2008 finale of *American Idol*, singing "Praying For Time," and the previous year embarked on a US tour for *Twenty Five*. "I'm there to absolutely acknowledge there are a million people in America that carried on seeking out my music even though it wasn't on the radio," he told *Spinner*, reflecting on the amount of time he'd been away. "And in a way, that's more special than anywhere else. I really didn't know I was going to be touring; that was something that only really occurred to me a couple of years ago. And yeah, ultimately, the truth is, the things that used to annoy me 'cause I'd lost them in America are actually not things I chase anymore. And I'm much less angry than I was; I was so angry in the '90s. I was just angry about losing my partner and losing my mother. Those feelings of anger are completely gone. I just understand it and I feel really blessed to be able to come back and I feel very blessed that the whole *Eli Stone* thing happened. I'm just much more positive about these things than I used to be."

But that was not the full story.

True to his promise, George released a new track on Christmas Day 2008, which was free to download from his website, although listeners were asked to make a donation to charity; it was "December Song" and perhaps because it was not possible to buy a physical copy of the single, it only made it to Number 14 in the UK charts. It too had an animated video, featuring George as a child. Ultimately, after he sang it on the 2009 series finale of *The X Factor*, physical copies were made and it was re-released commercially over Christmas for several years after that.

In 2009, George and Kenny Goss parted, although the news did not become public for another two years. George blamed the split on his issues with substance abuse: "My partner went through similar problems with drink," he told an audience in 2011. The split left George defenseless and alone. His emotional crutch had gone and by now it was extremely clear to just about everyone that he was far more vulnerable than he had originally appeared and desperately needed emotional support.

Later that year, George met the person who was to be his last regular companion: Fadi Fawaz, thirteen years his junior. An Australian-born photographer and celebrity hair stylist, mystery still surrounds a great deal of their relationship. The pair were first pictured together in 2015 and Fadi was certainly supportive when George was doing one of his various stints in rehab, as will be seen.

Meanwhile, George appeared to be putting his energies into his work. A tour of Australia followed—his first intwenty-two years—in 2010, and then, in 2011, came something that actually ended up as the inspiration for James Corden's hugely popular "Carpool Karaoke" segment on *The Late Late Show*. The idea came about as part of a sketch for Comic Relief, the annual UK charity telethon. George was going to issue a cover version of the New Order number "True Faith" but he was also asked to take part in an extended comedy sketch. "My original idea was to pick George Michael up from prison in a car," Corden told US talk-show host Stephen Colbert on *The Late Show*. "And then we realized, 'Maybe we'll lose the prison, but what if there's still some fun for me and George to be in the car and we'll sing some Wham! songs?'

The very fact that George was to make light of his brushes with the law, of which much more in the next chapter, was an indication that he did not take himself too seriously, and the eventual video showed a man who really was willing to take the piss out of himself. A star-studded cast included what seemed like a roll call of the British great and good in the main body of the sketch, but George was not part of them. Instead, he was James's mate in the car. On hearing that James ('Smithy' in the sketch) has been summoned to sort out the Comic Relief video, George asks if he can go too, only to be rebuffed with the words, "Comic Relief is for people like you." George sulks for a while ("Don't put on your sad face," James reprimands him) before being coaxed out of it to sing along to some Wham! numbers. He then obediently sits in the car until James finally reappears and the two of them drive off together, singing "I'm Your Man."

The sketch was wildly successful and enjoyed a significant afterlife. When Corden moved to the United States to host *The Late Late Show*, probably his most popular segment became "Carpool Karaoke," which he attributed directly to the "George effect." People had initially been hesitant to appear, until Mariah Carey saw George's performance: "If it's good enough for George, it's good enough for me," James recounted her saying.

There was another free download in April 2011, when George covered Stevie Wonder's "You And I" to mark the occasion of the wedding of Prince William and Kate Middleton, along with another request that downloaders make a contribution to charity.

George's last-ever tour was to be the Symphonica Tour, which kicked off in 2011. Originally, the tour, which primarily featured numbers from the *Songs From The Last Century* and *Patience* albums, had been planned to accompany the release of the former disc but had been shelved. However, after the huge success of the Twenty Five tour, the idea was revived and indeed, the moment it was announced, shows were added across the UK and Europe as fans bought the tickets as soon as they came up for sale. It was to take the form of an orchestral concert tour with a live orchestra, and many of the dates sold out immediately, but it was also to be the backdrop to the first serious intimations that George might be having problems with his health. In November 2011, he was in the Austrian capital of Vienna when he was taken to the hospital and discovered to be suffering a serious bout of pneumonia. Tour dates were postponed or, in the case of Australia, cancelled altogether.

By this stage the public had become unhappily aware that George Michael was having some very difficult trials in his personal life and initially it seemed as if this was just another crisis. Gradually, however, it became apparent that the problems were serious. In the last few years of his life, George didn't give many interviews, but he did reveal to his local paper in London, the *Ham & High*, that doctors had had to perform a tracheotomy: "It almost killed me," he said. "On a subconscious level it was very frightening and I'll probably never feel quite as safe again. But I was just so grateful to come out alive and get back to my home in London."

In the aftermath of the illness he was pictured looking extremely frail and badly shaken. The illness had affected his lungs, dangerous for anyone and a potential disaster for a singer. George cut down on his smoking but did not cut it out altogether and, shaken as he was, did not take this as a wake-up call, merely promising to get back out on the road again to make it up to the fans, which he did.

The depth of genuine affection towards him became

clear, however, when he appeared at the Brit Awards in February 2012, two months after he had left the hospital. He received a standing ovation and presented singer-songwriter Adele with an award for Best British album (for *21*).

*Symphonica*, the album, was released in March 2014 and went to Number 1 in the UK. In 2016, George announced that he would be taking part in a second documentary about his life, to be called *Freedom*. It was scheduled for release in March 2017.

# A MUCH-LOVED MAN

# 1 3

# DARKNESS
# FALLS

It was George himself who summed it up: "the lunacy."
He was certainly not alone among those rock stars
seeking oblivion in sex and drugs but, as he became
increasingly disillusioned by the world and lost or became
distant from so many of the people he cared about, he turned
increasingly to anonymous trysts and illicit substances.
And nothing anyone said or did could stop him. He seemed
absolutely set on a path to self-destruction and in the end,
sadly, he succeeded.

Ironically, matters seem to have got worse after he came
out. The young George was deeply unhappy not just at
having to hide his sexuality but, also, according to many
people who knew him, because in the early days he found
it very difficult to accept that he was gay. He wanted to
be like Andrew Ridgeley; he simply didn't want to be

George. In fact, he wasn't really George—he was Georgios Kyriacos Panayiotou, affectionately known to his nearest and dearest as "Yog," a shortening of the way his Greek name was pronounced. He was the product of a traditional Greek Cypriot household and that meant he would have found it extremely difficult as a young man to accept that he was gay.

When details began to emerge of George's numerous travails, the public mood was one of concern mixed with incomprehension. How could it possibly be that the golden boy of the eighties was turning into such a wreck? And it was in 2005, the year that he and Kenny Goss decided to put their civil partnership on hold, and the year in which he expressed such regret about the way his life had turned out in the documentary *George Michael: A Different Story*, that matters really started to get out of hand. In February 2006, George was arrested for possession of Class C drugs on a street near Hyde Park Corner in London, cautioned by the police and released.

The police released the details and, although the statement was itself issued in toned-down language, it painted a lurid picture of what had happened. "We were called by a member of the public to a man seen slumped over the steering wheel of a car on the street close to Hyde Park Corner," a police spokesman said. "An ambulance attended, but the man was not suffering from any injuries so was not conveyed to hospital. Police attended and spoke to the man, aged 42. A search of the man revealed what was believed to be controlled substances. He was arrested on suspicion of possession of controlled substances of category C and on suspicion of being unfit to drive. Following an examination by the duty doctor in the custody suite he was de-arrested for the driving offence. He has been released on bail to return to a central London police station on a date in late March pending analysis of the substances recovered."

After his previous arrest George made a video satirising the affair. This time he didn't, saying merely that it was "my own stupid fault as usual." It was a harbinger of more to come. Soon afterwards there were reports that he had hit three cars with his Range Rover and rather than stop to investigate, he just drove off. George was dismissive of the reports, appearing on *Parkinson* in April that year to declare that he was feeling better than he had in years. "I thought I'd hit one car," said George. "The papers say I rushed away and didn't tell anybody, which is rubbish. By the time I'd sent somebody to get details of what I thought was one incident, the *Daily Mail* was already there and, from that point, it just escalated. I had people frantically calling my house to find out whether I was in hospital and I literally just had a parking accident."

Presenter Michael Parkinson also asked him about the previous incident: "Are we really going to say that's dramatic?" said George. "I don't know how it happened. I guess it was momentary. I was at the lights with my foot still on the brake and I must have nodded off... of course they [the police] had to check out whether I was fit to drive because I was asleep."

George was accused of cruising for anonymous sex on Hampstead Heath by the now defunct *News of the World*. He reacted furiously, denying the encounter in question but angrily defending his lifestyle. He was particularly angry that the paper linked this to the postponement of the civil partnership with Kenny Goss. He was sick of the coverage of his private life, he said; sick of photographers harassing him—"I should not have to worry about who's watching me at two thirty in the morning"—and was pretty much pissed off about everything.

"I'm suing the individual involved who I have never, ever seen, let alone wanted to have any kind of sexual encounter with, and I'm currently investigating suing the secondary sources of libel," he told the BBC. "I have done nothing this year against the law, I've done nothing to encourage talk about my sex life. The question is not whether I bring it to the public, but it is why do I have to defend it in public because I don't want to talk about it at all. I don't know anybody who actually goes to Hampstead Heath at two o'clock in the morning for anything other than the reason of playing about with another member of the human race. If they are there, then they are a little bit strange or they just don't know the local area. A very large part of the male population, gay or straight, totally understands the idea of anonymous and no-strings sex. The fact that I choose to do that on a warm night in the best cruising ground in London—which happens to be about half a mile from my home—I don't think would be that shocking to that many gay people. Until such time as the straight world is not attacking people for cruising, I'd say the gay world could actually keep that to themselves, just for a little bit longer."

From then on, George just could not seem to keep out of the press for all the wrong reasons. He lost his driving license in 2007 after again being found slumped at the steering wheel of his car. He was banned from driving for two years. It mattered to him, though, that people realized this was connected to sleeping pills and not cannabis. "For all the doctored pictures, every single breathalyzer test I've taken in my life has read 0.0, and I've never failed a sobriety test," he told the *Guardian* in 2009. "I always preface this with, 'I deserved to lose my licence, I needed to lose my licence.' I had a problem with sleeping pills for about a year and a half, and I fucked up really badly. I got in the car twice when I'd forgotten I'd already downed something to try to get me to sleep. It doesn't matter that it wasn't deliberate—ultimately, I did it a second time, and I could have killed somebody. But the fact remains I was never accused of driving under the influence. I got done for exhaustion and sleeping pills."

Despite his protestations, George's drug use was heavy and he knew it. On the BBC's *Desert Island Discs* in September 2007, he said that he smoked far too much dope and wished he could cut down. "Absolutely I would like to take less, no question," he said. "To that degree, it's a problem." But it was not "getting in the way of my life in any way. I'm a happy man and I can afford my marijuana so that's not a problem." He was deluding himself. At its worst and by his own admission, he smoked up to twenty-five spliffs a day; when he cut back that went down to eight or nine, which was still a lot.

A year later he was back in the headlines after being arrested in a public loo on Hampstead Heath for possession of Class A and Class C drugs; another police caution followed. There was some criticism of the fact that he only received a caution, given that Class A drugs were now involved; that was also an indication that George was now dabbling in more dangerous substances. The rumor was that it was crack cocaine.

George did not learn his lesson. In 2009, he was arrested after his car hit a tractor-trailer on the A34, a major truck route in England. He was released without charge and later said he had been "stone cold sober" and didn't want his family to be "worried about what they were reading." In reality they must have been frantic. Lawrie Rowe was the driver of the tractor and said George must have been driving at about 100 miles an hour: "He came over to my cab and asked if I had stopped to give him a lift," he told the *Sun*. "He was absolutely not with it, so I told him 'no.' But he insisted and tried to get in. When it finally dawned on him that I wouldn't give in, he walked off."

This episode was absolutely perplexing to family, friends and fans alike. It wasn't as if George couldn't afford a taxi and at times it seemed that he was almost going out of his way to cause trouble for himself. Matters were shortly to get a whole lot worse. In the early hours of Sunday morning, at around 3.30 a.m. on July 4, 2010, he was on his way back from a Gay Pride march when he crashed his car into the front of a Snappy Snaps store in Hampstead. It was captured on CCTV and this time George did not get off so lightly, not least as this was the seventh time he had got into trouble with his car. "Police were called at approximately 3:30 a.m. on Sunday to reports of a vehicle in collision with a building," said a police spokesman. "Officers attended and a man in his 40s was arrested on suspicion of being unfit to drive. He was taken to a North London police station and later bailed to return during August pending inquiries." George was not breathalyzed but he was tested for drugs. A slightly bemused Snappy Snaps employee said, "The police have got the CCTV and the manager is dealing with it. No one knows what happened."

Of course, George's private life had become extremely turbulent by that stage. More than ever the emotional stability he had sought all his life eluded him. It didn't help when an extraordinary fight blew up involving Snappy Snaps itself: the damaged shop front was left as it was for some time, upsetting some of George's fans, who thought it was deliberate and being used to exploit the connection. They went so far as to send a letter to the local paper, the *Ham & High*: "We feel concerned that despite Mr Michael paying for the shop front to be repaired, the manager of the shop appears to be taking an extraordinary long time to get somebody to fix the damage. We would like to voice our concern that the manager of this particular branch is using what happened on the 4th July as a way to promote his shop." A spokesman for the branch somewhat wearily responded that it had been left as it was for insurance purposes. There was a further bizarre twist to all this: after George's death, fans left notes and flowers at the shop as some sort of shrine, leading to staff putting up a polite note to ask them to stop.

But concerned fans were not going to be able to help George after the actual incident. The case went to court and the lurid details were there for all to see: "The engine was still running," said prosecutor Penny Fergusson of what the police found when they arrived at the scene. "Officers saw Mr Michael slumped in the vehicle. When officers knocked on the window he jumped up. He was seen to be making movements, trying to get the car into gear. He looked at the officers with eyes wide open. He was dripping with sweat. Officers asked him to get out of the car but he remained where he was. They placed him in handcuffs. He still did not respond and, in their words, appeared to be spaced out. He had to be supported by the officers, who again noticed he was sweating and breathing heavily. When asked what had happened, he looked at the officers very confused. He said he did not do it and did not crash into anything."

In defense, George's lawyer, Mukul Chawla, QC, said that the singer had taken a sleeping pill, but the police had found two cannabis cigarettes in the car and there was cannabis in George's system. He was sentenced to eight weeks, a fine and banned from driving for five years. He was branded a drug addict by the Judge John Perkins: George Michael was a "risk to the public." He had taken a "dangerous and unpredictable mix" of prescription drugs and cannabis. "I accept entirely that you have shown remorse for the offense, that you are ashamed of it, that you admitted it. Despite the resources at your command it does not appear that you took proper steps to deal with what's clearly an addiction to cannabis."

George gasped and was in tears as the sentence was handed down, as indeed was Kenny Goss, who was also in court. Whatever the exact state of their relationship, he clearly still played a big part in George's life. George was taken to Pentonville prison, in North London—it had also played host to Boy George at one stage—a category B jail.

George was later moved to a category C jail, HMP Highpoint. One of the prison officers, Amanda Watts, sold information about him to the tabloids, including a sketch of the area around his cell; she was handed a prison sentence of twelve months as punishment. Meanwhile, Boy George, Elton John and Paul McCartney all wrote to George to offer their support.

George served four weeks before he was released; he later said that it had been a wake-up call and that was certainly the last time he crashed his car in such circumstances. "Pentonville was really quite a horrific experience, and I was put in with the pedophiles and the bullies, I suppose," he later told BBC Radio 2's *Chris Evans Breakfast Show* in a programme entitled *Up Close with George Michael*, broadcast in two parts on March 18 and 19, 2014. "I didn't leave my cell very much in those few days. From the moment that last crash happened (I started to get sober) —because apart from anything else, I realized it had to be something to do with me. It shook me out of my denial in a way that the others hadn't, probably because there was a chance I'd go to prison. So from the day after that crash happened, I started in drug counselling." His drug problems were now completely behind him, he added, although tragically this was to prove anything but the case.

He certainly seemed to feel that he deserved the sentence, telling presenter Chris Evans, "By the time I went to court, I knew this wasn't going to happen again. I knew I was going to lose my license. I was assured I wasn't going to prison but I thought I was and, like I said, it was much easier to take because I felt it was deserved. This was a hugely shameful thing to have done repeatedly so karmically I felt like I had a bill to pay. I went to prison, I paid my bill. Remarkably enough—I know people must think it was a really horrific experience—it's so much easier to take any form of punishment if you believe you actually deserve it, and I did."

As for his first night: "Well, it was Pentonville. It wasn't a weekend break, put it that way. What did I think? Well, I didn't feel sorry for myself. I thought, 'Oh my God, this place is absolutely filthy,' because it was Pentonville. I just thought, 'You get your head down.' Those stories of me crying are rubbish. They wish that was me, but that's not me."

On his last night in prison, "every single staff member" and prisoner got his autograph, some on headed prison paper. "This guy comes in with a guitar and he said he wanted me to write the date. So I asked the date, and he said it's the 10th of the 10th of the 10th. And I just thought, 'That's so fitting.' It's kind of like the clock rolling round to the end of something, tomorrow I start again."

Ultimately, alas, it was an opportunity to clean up that was missed. That was the end of the drug-driving, but it was by no means the end either of drugs or problems involving cars. Kicking the habit turned out to be only temporary and George's use of cannabis was soon on the up again, something many suspected was behind a bizarre accident on May 16, 2013. He was a passenger in a Range Rover on the M1 when there was some sort of a crash at ten to six in the afternoon at junction 6A, near St Albans, in Hertfordshire. An ambulance was called: "The man who we believe to be in his 40s sustained a head injury and following treatment, stabilization and immobilization by land and air ambulance crews, he was flown to hospital for further care," said ambulance spokesman Gary Sanderson.

A police spokesman added, "The exact circumstances of what happened are unclear at this time and until further investigations have been carried out it would be inappropriate for us to comment further."

What actually happened was later confirmed by Katherine Fox, who had been driving behind George's car and screeched to a halt in her Mini in a bid to protect him. He had fallen out of the car and was in a bad way: "There was a nasty cut on his forehead and the back of his head," she told the *Sun*. "There was blood all down his face and on his teeth. He was breathing and conscious, but in shock." His tracksuit had been ripped and trainers had come off.

The question, of course, was how on earth did this happen? George's people explained that his car door had not been properly closed and when trying to adjust it, he fell out, but that did beg the question as to why he waited until he was on the motorway to try to fix the problem. There was a great deal of speculation that George had done it deliberately; in the wake of George's death his former lover Fadi Fawaz seemed to say that George had previously tried to commit suicide and then said that he had implied no such thing and his Twitter account had been hacked. Whatever the exact truth, it certainly indicated a very troubled state of mind and there were also reports that the singer had once slashed his wrists. He had certainly never hidden the fact that he had struggled with depression for about twenty years.

George was kept in the hospital for a few days and emerged mercifully unscathed in the longer term but behind the scenes he was deteriorating. In 2013, he spent some time in the Sanctuary, an Australian $42,000-a-week rehab clinic. Fadi was around at the time, although he said he was not staying in the clinic himself but visiting his mother in Queensland. George was said to be suffering from emotional anxiety and a posting on his website in September 2012 had certainly acknowledged that something was wrong: "I'm afraid I believed (wrongly) that making music and getting out there to perform for the audiences that bring me such joy would be therapy enough in itself. Unfortunately I seriously underestimated how difficult this year would be and although I was right to believe that the shows would bring me great happiness and that my voice would recover completely (I truly think that some of my recent performances have been my best ever) I was wrong to think I could work my way through the major anxiety that has plagued me since I left Austria last December."

While in Australia, George had a brief encounter with a Columbian hairdresser called Carlos Arturo Ortiz, who gave an insight into the singer's state of mind at the time. "I found him a lovely, down-to-earth man, but also a very melancholic person who I feared might one day take his own life," he told the *Sunday People*. "He told me he was addicted to anti-depressant medicine and trying to wean himself off it and confessed he was unhappy. We talked about his superstar status and I told him I thought that with his fame and talent and money he had all he needed to be happy in life. But when he started talking about the anti-depressants he took I asked him outright if he was happy in life and he replied, 'No, I'm not.'" Carlos also saw George putting drops into a bottle of water before downing them: "I knew they were drugs, but I didn't ask him what they were and we never talked about it," he said. "They didn't alter his mood particularly. All he drank apart from the champagne was Coca-Cola, which he told me he downed by the gallon and was addicted to, along with chocolate." That would have explained the weight gain, although when Carlos met him George was still in good shape.

But George's troubles were running deep now. In 2014, an ambulance was called to his home. Although the incident was played down, his family could only look on aghast. In 2015, Jackie Georgiou, the wife of George's cousin, Andros, went public to the *Sun on Sunday*, revealing that George was taking hard drugs. "He was smoking crack. Before he went away, he'd got to the point where he would be shaking, saying: 'I need it,'" she said. "There were parties where he was taking drugs and collapsing and being picked up off the floor. Waking up in vomit, horrible things. He was so thin, so ill. It's crack, it's marijuana, it's drink, it's coke. It was pretty dark and things were getting darker. He was going to end up locked up or dead. I'm petrified he will die."

He certainly wasn't thin at the end, but he was in a dreadful state. "He's a very addictive person," Jackie continued. "He was always sneaking off [for sex]. It got riskier and riskier. It was not just in bathrooms, it was in bushes and parks. In the end, there were rent boys involved, and that's when he got heavily into the drug use."

According to *NME*, a spokesperson for George said this was "highly inaccurate. These stories have been apparently provided to the Press by the wife of a very distant family member, neither of whom has had any dealings with him for many years. It is therefore unsurprising they are so incorrect."

George and Andros had indeed fallen out years previously, but the fact was that in 2015, George checked into rehab in a final attempt to recover his health. He was treated at the Kusnacht Practice, just outside Zurich; at the time the fees were said to be £200,000–£280,000. When the reports first surfaced, George did a disappearing act: "He came to Switzerland because he wanted to kick a drug habit," a source close to the clinic told the *Daily Mail*. "He picked the one place in the world that takes individualism to new heights—they have no more than three people under care at any one time. But he has gone to ground since the news of his latest therapy broke. The word is he wants to let the media storm die down before he goes back in for more treatment."

Could the clinic help where all else had failed? "It is the norm at most addiction clinics to treat people like prisoners, to isolate them from the temptations that have dragged them off the straight and narrow," said the source. But the Kusnacht doesn't do this. Its philosophy is that the outside world has to be faced when the touchy-feely part is over and the client is dispatched to the real world. George had a chauffeur at his disposal to take him wherever he wanted to go, to do whatever he wanted to do. In the aftermath of his death, it emerged that George had in fact spent months in the clinic, although he never revealed whether he was being treated for depression, drug addiction, or both.

At the time, though, his people denied that he was currently in rehab but left it open as to whether he had just finished a stint at the clinic: "We do not comment on private and confidential matters, such as anything related to previous medical treatment George may or may not have received—and we also expect you to respect his rights of privacy in such matters. However, we can say that contrary to some of the reports in the Press, George has not just entered rehab but is spending time in Europe. He is well and enjoying an extended break, as the recent photographs in a national newspaper clearly illustrate."

Later photographs charted a massive physical change. Apart from his heavy drug use—and reports of heroin consumption, while denied by his family, continued to circulate—George was also eating far too much and by the time of his death bore little resemblance to the handsome star he had once been. Rare pictures of him emerged, looking tired and bloated. As mentioned earlier, the manager of his local pub in Oxfordshire commented anonymously, "He had changed over the years, got a lot bigger and wore glasses. He was very self-conscious. He just did not look like George Michael any more." And the fall from the car had made matters worse: George was by all accounts worried about the appearance of his scars. And in the run-up to his death he had clearly gained a huge amount of weight: the last pictures of him (which were taken when he was having dinner with friends, including Kenny Goss) revealed as much. But still no one expected the worst: George had survived so much previously, how could he not do so again?

# 1 4

# FRIENDS AND
# FALL-OUTS

George Michael spent his entire adult life mixing with his fellow great and good and in the course of it got involved in various friendships and fall-outs—sometimes with the same people—which could be rather confusing to the outside world. One minute he could be best friends with Elton John; the next they were distanced. Nonetheless, his friendships were clearly important to him, none more so than his relationship with Andrew Ridgeley.

Some of his childhood friends dropped by the wayside but shared memories of George after he died. One was a schoolmate called Penny Ling, who discovered poems written by 11-year-old Georgios, as he then was, in her school yearbook from 1974 when they both attended Roe Green Junior School. Penny had been a couple of years below George, while her sister had been in the same class as George's sister Melanie.

"My sister had recognized his sister at an awards ceremony George Michael was attending, and came back and said, 'You will never guess who I met,'" she told the *Mirror*. "I think she got his autograph. At the time my sister was a buyer at Tesco and she got taken to the ceremony by one of her customers. When she told me, I then went to my 1974 yearbook and looked through it and lo and behold, there were two poems from George Michael. The whole school was represented in the book. It was published once a year. The only people that know about it were friends of mine who were massive George Michael fans. I kept my yearbook locked away in a cupboard.

"For an eleven-year-old I think the way it's written is quite complex. He was a couple of years above me."

Penny thinks it might have been an exceptional teacher that spurred George on. "Back then we had the same teacher called Mr Ian Greenwood, who taught creative writing," she recalled. "I wonder whether part of George's significant writing ability stems from that class. The reason I remember him is he lived at the back of my best friend's house in Burnt Oak, London. The whole area was very multi-national. George Michael's family were not the only Cypriots living in that community, it was a real mixed bag. I lived the opposite end of the school catchment area. I would go round to [my] friend's house maybe once a month. She lived in a cul-de-sac and over the back was a bit of wasteland and sometimes we would play in the cul-de-sac if we needed a hard surface—George Michael joined in. We would play cowboys and Indians, pogo-sticking—how long you could bounce on a stick without falling off—hopscotch, the usual kids' games. I probably knew him from about six to nine years old, so he would have been nine to eleven roughly. I found him to be one of these people to be reasonably quiet and studious. He absorbed what was going on around him. He was not a flash person or didn't like to show off. He didn't stand out as… exceptional or different. He was just like the rest of us."

The childhood friendships that lasted were extremely important to George. Towards the end of his life, he became very reclusive and saw only a close circle from the early days, already charted in this book. But one enduring relationship, only briefly mentioned to date, was with David Austin, originally known as David Mortimer, who George referred to as his best friend in *George Michael: A Different Story*, the 2005 documentary. The two of them went back a long way. Born in 1962, David was a a member of The Executives, and had a hit himself in 1984, called "Turn To Gold," which was co-written with George and on which George sang backing vocals. This turned into a long-term songwriting partnership, including "You Have Been Loved" and "Look At Your Hands" from *Faith*, as well as "John and Elvis Are Dead" and "December Song." The latter nearly ended up as a Spice Girls' offering.

"I started writing the song in my own home studio back in 2006," David told the *Sunday Mirror*. "George liked the chorus and we began working on it together. George's partner Kenny Goss played it to the Spice Girls' manager Simon Fuller and singer Geri Halliwell, and they immediately wanted it for a Christmas album. But the song still wasn't properly finished and George was off on tour, with no free time to return to the recording studio. So the Spice Girls never got it. As the song progressed, we then thought of giving it to Michael Buble. But George decided he was going to keep it for himself."

David remained extremely close to George throughout his life and was one of the few people who saw him regularly at the end. He had a ringside seat during his friend's travails: recalling his bout of pneumonia, he said, "It was touch and go. We were all very worried, as you would be with a family member." When the ambulance incident happened in 2014, David arrived and set about rebuffing reporters at George's home: "It's just ridiculous what's happening," he said. "He's not ill. He's been mixing his record over the weekend, he's perfectly fine. We've been working down at Air Studios round the corner in Hampstead, that's where we do all the recordings. He's been mixing his demo tape over the weekend." Pointing to a package he was carrying, he added: "Look, here's the demo. We'll be having a listen to it now." But despite all attempts to downplay George's problems, by this time they were clearly beginning to take hold.

That mention of the Spice Girls hinted at another intimate. One of George's more surprising friendships was with Geri Halliwell as she was then (now Geri Horner after her marriage in 2015 to Christian Horner, the head of the Red Bull F1 racing team). The two became close in the late 1990s, around the time that Geri left the Spice Girls, and for a few years were frequently pictured together, although the friendship waned over time.

Indeed, it turned out that initially Geri wanted a good deal more than friendship. George had been her childhood crush. "I'm totally off. My gaydar is useless—well, it's better these days," she told the *Sun*. "With George Michael years ago I'd made plans to marry him, I used to practice kissing with his poster. Then we met and I started being all flirty eyes, licking my lips and the sexy poses and I just felt there was nothing coming back. Then I was chatting on the phone to him and he starts talking about his boyfriend and I'm like 'What? How could I be so wrong!'"

That misunderstanding cleared up, they went on to form a bond. Geri stayed with George in LA, and it was during a visit to Goring-on-Thames made by the two of them that George decided to buy a house in the area on the grounds that no one had recognized him. And of course they both worked in the music industry, so they understood the stresses and strains each felt. "You know he's the only celebrity friend I have, aside from the Spice Girls, that I tell all my secrets to," Geri continued. "I have long chats with him, he's like a brother. In the past I've played my music to him and sometimes he'd tell me it's shit and other times it's great. He's very normal when you talk one-on-one with him."

But there were strains. For a year or two the pair seemed to spend their whole time in each other's company, as a friend noted: "George was a fantastic friend to Geri over the years and supported her through some tough times." The singer himself finally said something on the subject, in an interview with Jo Whiley on BBC Radio 1 in March 2002: "Geri's a lovely girl. But it's very difficult to maintain a relationship with a person who lives for the press."

When Geri gave birth to her daughter Bluebell by screenwriter Sacha Gervasi in 2006, Kenny Goss was named as the godfather. When Geri got married to Formula One's Christian Horner in May 2015, George was not there, because of his poor state of health.

George had a very up-and-down relationship with Sir Elton John. They had a good deal in common, both being entertainers who were initially believed to be straight and had to come out in the public eye; both also had problems with drug use. Both also did a lot for charities, especially those related to HIV/AIDS. But Sir Elton famously overcame his addictions and settled into a lengthy and stable relationship with filmmaker David Furnish. George never managed to do either.

George was an early Elton fan—he and Andrew Ridgeley had listened to *Goodbye Yellow Brick Road* together as children—and later contributed backing vocals to two of his mid-1980s hits, "Nikita" and "Wrap Her Up." That same year, 1985, he also sang Elton's 1974 hit, "Don't Let The Sun Go Down On Me" during the Live Aid concert, with Elton accompanying him on piano, a double act they repeated at George's Wembley Arena concert in 1991. The duet was recorded and released as a single towards the end of that year; it got to Number 1 in both the UK and US.

But matters seemed to change, ironically around the time that George came out, and by 2004 the rift had gone public. Elton gave an interview in which he spoke of George being "in a strange place" and that there was "deep-rooted unhappiness" in his life, which was quite true, if a little tactless. He further stated that George was smoking far too much cannabis and that the album *Patience* wasn't very good. George was livid: "Elton knows very little about George Michael and that's a fact," he snapped. "Most of what Elton knows about my life is limited to the gossip he hears on the gay grapevine." Elton still relied on his old hits, he added, while his own "passion and drive is about the future."

In 2006, when he appeared on *Parkinson*, George went a lot further, naming this incident as the moment when the real problems began. He blamed Elton for what was now becoming years of negative press coverage: "The trajectory of my particular soap opera launched from that statement Elton made about eighteen months ago when Elton hadn't seen me in years. The subtext to it is he was all right before he came out and now he lives this depraved gay life and he's miserable and fat. Elton said he thought I was really miserable for some reason. From that point on, I've been trying to prove that I'm not." It is thought that Elton, who knew all about the dangers of drug use and life in the public eye, was trying to establish contact behind the scenes, but to no avail.

By 2009, matters had deteriorated further. As recorded by Simon Hattenstone in an interview for the *Guardian* in December that year, George burst out: "Elton lives on that. He will not be happy until I bang on his door in the middle of the night saying, 'Please, please, help me, Elton. Take me to rehab.' It's not going to happen. You know what I heard last week? That Bono... Oh for God's sake... Geri told Kenny that Bono, having spoken to Elton, had approached Geri to say, 'What can we do for George?' This is what I have to deal with because I don't want to be part of that social clique. All I'd have to do to stop it is hang out in London, so people realize I don't look close to death... As if Bono gives a shit what I do with my private life... Elton just needs to shut his mouth and get on with his own life. Look, if people choose to believe that I'm sitting here in my ivory tower, Howard Hughesing myself with long fingernails and loads of drugs, then I can't do anything about that, can I?"

There was another intemperate blast in 2011, as recorded in several papers, including the *Evening Standard* and the *Daily Mail*—"We all earn the right to get a little more grumpy as we get older," said George, "but he's [Elton] getting terribly close to Nan territory, you know, the Nan from *Catherine Tate*." It is clear that Elton was motivated by a true affection for George and attempted to save him from his own demons, though his methods were questionable. Later the same year, George agreed to appear in a concert for the Elton John Aids Foundation and Elton made a point of thanking him publicly: "George has been a patron of the Foundation since its inception and has been a much-valued supporter over the years, as well as a dear friend. This is an incredible and generous gesture. I thank George from my heart for doing this. His is an amazing talent, and this is a fantastic gift he is making to people affected by HIV."

From then on it was all smiles, but of course Elton was to be vindicated in a way that devastated him and everyone else. After George's body was found he posted a picture of the two of them sitting at a piano: "I am in deep shock," he wrote. "I have lost a beloved friend—the kindest, most generous soul and a brilliant artist. My heart goes out to his family and all of his fans. #RIP." He followed that up by saying that George was "one of the kindest, sweetest, most generous people" he'd ever met and that his death was "one of the saddest moments." A couple of days later, in Las Vegas at a concert in Caesar's Palace, with a large projection of George behind him, an emotional Elton sang "Don't Let The Sun Go Down On Me," adding, "I only wish George was here to sing it with me."

Chris Stacey, of London, was in the audience, and told DailyMail.com: "There were thousands of us in tears and it was very emotional. Elton had sung a song in memory of John Lennon when he spoke about George Michael. After he sang for George, he turned his back on the audience and was shaking and looked like he was crying. I was in tears and so was everyone around me. He received a standing ovation and had to be consoled by a band member before beginning the rest of the show. There wasn't a dry eye in the house." Elton's grief spoke volumes. After all, he had known George from the beginning, when he was still very much the golden boy.

George and Boy George came to prominence around the same time in the 1980s, but their images could not have been more different—gorgeous George the golden boy on the one hand, surrounded by female admirers, and dreadlocked, made-up Boy George on the other, an altogether more eccentric presence on the scene.

Neither was out initially, but the Boy had always been a lot more out there than George and it didn't come as a great surprise to anyone when it emerged he was gay. He also had well-documented problems with drugs. But—he was not alone in the gay community in thinking this—he resented the fact that he had come out when George was still coming across as a ladies' man. "People saw me as the benchmark queer while George Michael was passing himself off as a straight stud," George complained to the *Evening Standard* in March 2005. "In fact, he was loitering in public loos like some pre-war homosexual. It's one thing to keep quiet, it's another to pretend you're someone you're not."

That was unfair: Boy George had never been a teen pin-up in the way that George Michael had been and George found himself in a very difficult position in the 1980s. But he was perfectly capable of holding his own in a war of words. "Boy George is great company and a man I have always wanted to like," he said icily. "He acts in a homophobic way to other gay men by being such a bitch. It's an aggression that he can't get rid of."

In the wake of the drug revelations, Boy George sounded a lot more sympathetic, however. He had had his own problems, addictions and a spell in prison, and knew what it was like to deal with such issues in the public eye. "I don't really see George Michael but we have exchanged emails recently and things are pretty good between us. He seems to be doing okay right now," he said in 2010, as quoted in the March 15 edition of *Pink News*. "You don't really tend to offer it [advice]—but I might give it, if asked."

He too was saddened by George's death. "I am thinking of George Michael's family, friends and fans right now," he tweeted once the news had become public. "He was so loved and I hope he knew it because the sadness today is beyond words. Devastating. What a beautiful voice he had and his music will live on as a testament to his talent. I can't believe he is gone. I hope the Buddha will hold him in his arms. NMRK [a reference to a Buddhist chant]."

As well as establishing fall-outs and friendships, by the end of his life George had also assumed the status of an elder statesman in the pop community, who had seen it all and done it all and was there to warn newcomers of the pitfalls—much as Frank Sinatra had done for him when he was younger. This was particularly the case when it came to other gay entertainers. When the singer Will Young, the first-ever winner of *Pop Idol*, came out in 2002, George was asked on BBC Radio 1 if he was surprised: "Oh, come on! I don't want to be insulting, but about as surprised as people were with me—and they had eighteen years to work on it."

But he followed that up with some wise words and they had nothing to do with sexuality: "I'd give them [Will Young and runner-up Gareth Gates] one very strong piece of advice," he said and given his own wrangles over contracts over the years, he clearly knew what he was talking about. "It is possible to weather the storm, but you need to make sure that the advice you're getting is completely disconnected from the people immediately around you, i.e. the people involved in that show. I would say to Gareth and Will that you have to understand that, although it's nice to believe different, the people in your immediate vicinity do not have your best interests at heart. If you need legal advice or musical advice about your future, you need to find it from someone who is a non-involved party because the people immediately around you see you as a quick way to make some money. Understand that you should enjoy this period of time and try to survive it, but don't look to the people immediately close to you on how to survive it."

It was good advice. But what, really, was the legacy George left?

# 15

# GEORGE REMEMBERED

George Michael might have gone many decades before his time, never able to escape the depression and drug addiction that set in after the tragedies of the early 1990s, but the work he did and the legacy he left will live on. Many of those who met him, especially in the early days, remember a fun, light-hearted George, a world away from the troubled figure of the later years, happy and carefree, with everything to live for.

John Blake, the publisher and erstwhile *Sunday People* editor, launched the "Bizarre" column at the *Sun* in 1982, which focused on celebrity news, before moving to the *Daily Mirror*, where he was assistant editor and launched a pop-music column called "White Hot Club." He spent a lot of time with George and Andrew Ridgeley during the Wham! days and remembers meeting them after a gig in

Glasgow, which they performed in their trademark shorts and summer clothes. "I got on very well with both of them," he recalls. "They were wide-eyed and so sweet."

The boys asked John to accompany them on a trip to Florida, giving him a Sony Walkman and a cassette tape to listen to on the plane. The cassette was a recording of "Wake Me Up Before You Go-Go" and John knew immediately it was going to be a hit. "They had an incredible relationship together and George was truly happy back then," he says. "We went out to Fort Lauderdale in a limo because George and Andrew loved to go out dancing and everyone got a bit drunk. This was a time of some tensions between America and Iran and Andrew, who looks a bit Arabic, stood on the seat of the limo with his head out through the open top and said, 'I am Iranian. I am here to bomb you.' Had they not broken up, I'm sure George wouldn't have had so many problems. Behind the scenes, George was actually quite shy and he hero-worshipped Andrew, who was just effervescent."

George could be a little difficult too: when Andrew refused to leave the disco where they had been dancing, George commandeered the limo and went back to the hotel by himself, leaving the rest of the party stranded. But that tricksiness had nothing to do with Wham!. John Blake remembers a conversation with the boys' then manager, Simon Napier-Bell, on the subject of "Careless Whisper," which, with its themes of longing, misery and regret, is an extraordinarily mature piece for a teenage boy to have written.

John was one of the judges for the 1985 Ivor Novello Awards and George won two that year, for Songwriter of the Year and Most Performed Work, which was "Careless Whisper." "At that point, George was very popular, but he still wasn't being taken too seriously," says John. "But that night, Elton John was sitting at our table and he told me, 'George Michael is probably the greatest songwriter of his generation. I write songs for a living, but he has a quite extraordinary talent.'" John introduced the extremely shy George to Elton, the very first time they met. He also arranged for Andrew to get membership for Tramp, then the most famous and exclusive nightclub in London, because Ridgeley, now a famous pop star, wanted a beautiful girlfriend and that was where they all went.

But John also accompanied the two on their tour of China in 1985 and was aware immediately that something had changed. "It had all gone wrong," he says. "Andrew wanted to leave and George was distraught. Andrew wanted a quieter life and they were arguing in rehearsals and shouting at one another. They went from being sweet and happy to really disillusioned. That is when George's dark and serious side caught up with him."

Without Andrew, George was never able to recapture that early happiness, while Andrew watched in dismay, from afar, as his old friend's life began to go into freefall. But George's impact on popular culture cannot be overstated and neither can his generosity. His extensive charitable donations were referred to in the first chapter of this book, but while many pop stars donate money, there are very few (if indeed any other than George) who go to the time and trouble of putting on a free concert to thank a group of people, as George did in 2006 when he staged a concert at The Roundhouse in North London to thank the nurses who had cared for his mother. He invited 2,000 members of the audience, while he was introduced on stage by the comedienne Catherine Tate. The place was "full of heroes," he said. "Society calls what you do a vocation, and that means you don't get paid properly. Thank you for everything you do—some people appreciate it. Now if we can only get the government to do the same thing."

The nurses queued up to show their appreciation: "Absolutely amazing night, made me feel appreciated and what a way to be thanked for doing my job. George was on top form and what a performance," wrote Sue Martin from Torquay on the BBC website. "A fantastic performance and atmosphere. So generous of George Michael. We really appreciated his actions, comments and generosity," added Kate Laycock from Shrewsbury.

His exceptional generosity stood out because he not only supported causes and the big charities, but individuals in need of help too. Some of it was detailed in the first chapter of this book, but there were numerous other examples as well, involving individuals who would otherwise have had nowhere to turn. For example, Jo Maidment appeared on ITV's *This Morning* in 2010 to talk about her difficulties in conceiving a child; she was not eligible for fertility treatment on the NHS, she explained, as her partner already had a daughter. Soon afterwards an anonymous donor contacted the program and said he would fund the treatment.

"I was home for two days and got a phone call from a personal assistant saying a businessman would like to donate some money for one cycle of IVF for you," she told the same program after she was invited back to talk about what had happened in the wake of George's death (and with his family's permission). "I didn't believe it at first... And it took me a good few days to respond because that wasn't what I came on the show for; I wanted to help other people in my position. But then we agreed to it, because [the PA, Michelle] said it was what this particular man wanted."

But George didn't leave it at that: "It was a couple of days after we came home with Betsy and we had loads of cards and flowers," Jo recalled. "There was a massive bouquet of flowers that came and I read the card that said, 'Congratulations to you both. Lots of love to Betsy. Love from Michelle [Michael's PA] and George Michael (AKA Anonymous) xx.' Me and my husband read it hundreds of times to believe it." Unsurprisingly, she was enormously saddened by George's death: "I cannot ever thank him enough for what he has done for me and my husband," she said. Again, this involved a personal effort on George's part on behalf of an individual and with no thought of the greater glory, not something to be found in abundance in the pop world.

And George's influence was felt far beyond the pop world. There was fashion too: in September 2016 US *Vogue* celebrated the twenty-sixth anniversary of "Freedom! '90" that October by remaking it with a host of contemporary models, including Adriana Lima, Joan Smalls, Taylor Hill, Anna Ewers and Irina Shayk. There is also an argument that by giving the assembled supermodels his voice, George was drawing attention away from their appearance, which is what they were usually judged on. He also made an impact with his own appearance, from the golden-boy era of Wham! to the "Choose Life" T-shirts to the leather-jacketed style icon to the trademark oversize earring in a way that most other major stars in his league have not done. Perhaps the only other two to have done so are Michael Jackson and Madonna.

George also played a role in changing the relationship between China and the West. Pop music is now widely listened to in China and the young Chinese are far more aware of Western popular culture than they were before Wham! toured there in the mid-1980s. It took courage for George and Andrew to go there; no one else had done it before.

George's duets and his music videos have lasted. So has the music itself, including the early Wham! tunes that were so often treated as musical bubble gum. George is regularly referenced in other art forms: in the sublime comedy *Arrested Development*, one of the characters is called George Michael Bluth (George after his grandfather;

Michael after his father) and in the first three exceptional series of the show, it is never, ever commented upon that he shares his name with a famous star. (In the fourth series, when it is noted, the humor is conspicuous by its absence.)

And in the BBC television soap *EastEnders*, Heather Trott, played by Cheryl Fergison, is obsessed with George Michael and names her son after him. George also made numerous TV cameos, including in *Extras*, *Little Britain* and *The Catherine Tate show*. And, of course, there was *Eli Stone*. His music, most specifically "Wake Me Up Before You Go-Go," was also played in one of the most famous scenes from the original *Zoolander* movie: when a group of male models accidentally hose each other down with gasoline—and then go up in flames.

George's image and his music dominate the indie film *Keanu*: "The way it was described to me was that [George Michael] was so cool that even drug lords got a tattoo of him," George's manager Michael Lippman told *Billboard* in April 2016. "[Comedy duo and filmmakers Key's and Peele's] characters go from quiet, unassuming guys to street thugs and they wanted to show something that didn't seem right, but when put into that situation, works perfectly. They chose him to be this character because of what his music meant and they turned George into a cool badass."

But above all, it is the case that George Michael sold 100 million records in his lifetime and, like other greats who went before their time, including Michael Jackson, Elvis, Prince,

Leonard Cohen, David Bowie and John Lennon, his music looks set to live far beyond his own lifetime. As he himself saw it, he stuck up for and to a certain extent reinvented the genre of music that made his name: "If you listen to a Supremes record or a Beatles record, which were made in the days when pop was accepted as an art of sorts, how can you not realize that the elation of a good pop record is an art form?" he asked *Rolling Stone* back in January 1988. "Somewhere along the way, pop lost all its respect. And I think I kind of stubbornly stick up for all of that."

George Michael was an extremely complicated man, tortured by an unhappy childhood and an inability to come to terms with his sexuality, but he was able to turn this inner turmoil into music that spoke to generations. His inability to find lasting happiness in his lifetime struck a chord with many people too: George showed that you could have all the money and success in the world and yet that was no guarantee of inner happiness. Whether his work was youthful, happy, political, assertive or melancholic, he spoke to millions, who identified with his output. George Michael, the man, may have gone, but George Michael, the music, will live on for many years to come.

# ACKNOWLEDGEMENTS

Many thanks to my inestimable publisher John Blake not only for publishing the book itself, but also for the invaluable insight into George Michael's early life. And thanks to my wonderful and patient editor Toby Buchan for all his work on the book.

**Emily Herbert** is a very experienced author and journalist. She has written biographies of numerous celebrities and contributed to a range of national newspapers. Emily is based in London and her hobbies are ballet, yoga and travel.

Other books by Emily Herbert:

*Robin Williams: When the Laughter Stops*
*Eddie Redmayne: The Biography*
*Piers Morgan: The Biography*
*Sir Terry Wogan: A Life of Laughter*
*Stephen Gately and Boyzone – Blood Brothers*
*Lady Gaga: Queen of Pop*
*Take That and Robbie Williams – Back for Good*
*Matt Smith: The Biography*
*Michael Jackson – King of Pop*